Science and Religion

Professor Lawrence M. Principe

THE TEACHING COMPANY ®

PUBLISHED BY:

THE TEACHING COMPANY
4840 Westfields Boulevard, Suite 500
Chantilly, Virginia 20151-2299
1-800-TEACH-12
Fax—703-378-3819
www.teach12.com

ISBN 1-59803-133-3

Lawrence M. Principe, Ph.D.

Professor of History of Science and Technology and of Chemistry,
Johns Hopkins University

Lawrence Principe did his undergraduate work at the University of Delaware, where he received a B.S. in chemistry and a B.A. in liberal studies in 1983. During this time, he developed his interest in the history of science, particularly the history of alchemy and early chemistry. He then entered the graduate program in chemistry at Indiana University, Bloomington, where he worked on the synthesis of natural products. Immediately upon completing the Ph.D. in organic chemistry (1988), he reentered graduate school, this time in history of science at Johns Hopkins University, and earned a Ph.D. in that field in 1996.

Since 1989, Professor Principe has taught organic chemistry at Johns Hopkins University. In 1997, he earned an appointment in history of science. Currently, he enjoys a split appointment as professor between the two departments, dividing his teaching equally between the two at both graduate and undergraduate levels. He also enjoys annoying safety inspectors by performing alchemical experiments in his office.

In 1999, Professor Principe was chosen as the Maryland Professor of the Year by the Carnegie Foundation; in 1998, he received the Templeton Foundation's award for courses on science and religion; and in 2004, he was the first recipient of the prestigious Francis Bacon Award for History and Philosophy of Science. He has also won several teaching awards bestowed by Johns Hopkins University.

Professor Principe's interests cover the history of science of the early modern and late medieval periods and focus particularly on the history of alchemy and chemistry. His first book was entitled *The Aspiring Adept: Robert Boyle and His Alchemical Quest* (1998), and he has since collaborated on a book on 17th-century laboratory practices (*Alchemy Tried in the Fire*, winner of the 2005 Pfizer Prize) and on a study of the image of the alchemist in Netherlandish genre paintings (*Transmutations: Alchemy in Art*). He is currently at work on a long-term study of the chemists at the Parisian Royal Academy of Sciences around 1700.

Table of Contents
Science and Religion

Science and Religion

Scope:

Science and religion are unquestionably two of the most potent forces that have shaped—and continue to shape—human civilization. How have these powerful forces interacted over time? What are the bases, terms, and varieties of their interactions? Popular opinion generally assumes an antagonistic relationship between the two, but modern scholarship increasingly reveals this as a one-sided view that is not only relatively recent but also self-servingly propagated to this day by extremist voices in both the religion and the science camps. This course's approach to the issue is both historical and philosophical. It examines several historical episodes that highlight features of "science and religion" and analyzes in context the questions and issues that these episodes raise.

We begin by probing the very nature of science and religion: How are they different and how are they similar in terms of their questions, methods, and sources of knowledge and certainty? Science and theology turn out to have more in common than is generally believed. Thereafter, we examine various models that have been proposed for the interactions between science and religion and reveal the political origins of the still-popular *warfare thesis*. The course then embarks on a largely chronological study of important and illustrative episodes. These episodes include the famous cases of Galileo Galilei's moving Earth and the (continuing) fallout from Charles Darwin's theory of evolution, as well as issues relating to the age of the Earth and the origin of life. We will also examine notions regarding the level of God's involvement in the running of the cosmos; the roles of miracles, angels, and demons; and the problems of correctly identifying them. We will look at varieties of biblical interpretation and the highly varied readings of biblical narratives (especially Genesis 1) in different epochs and among different denominations, as well as the rise and fall of natural theology and its modern cousin, *intelligent design*. Our sources will be not only historical, scientific, and theological texts but also recent documents and events that serve to bring our discussions down to the present day.

Throughout the course, historical episodes are placed in their proper context and closely analyzed as we endeavor to get at the real issues involved. In some cases, we discover that the issues were not actually science and religion interactions, and in other cases, we find some issues that remain unresolved today, no matter how much partisans of rigidly scientific and rigidly religious viewpoints try to overlook them. Throughout, we will see how the strict division of "scientific" and "religious" thought is a modernism that cannot be "read back" into history. Indeed, much of the course reveals science and theology, faith and reason, as two individually incomplete methods—sometimes harmonious, sometimes not—that human beings have used in their endless quest for understanding.

Lecture One
Science and Religion

Scope:

In this introductory lecture, we define the basic terms of the course, its content, methodology, and focus. This course deals with the interactions of Christianity with science in the Western world over a long time span. We also look more closely at the terms *science* and *religion* in order to prepare ourselves for consistent discussions in future lectures. Finally, we look briefly at the various models for the interactions of science and religion that have been proposed, critique them, and provide some pointers for engaging with the balance of the course.

Outline

I. Science and religion are two of the most important influences on human civilization.

    A. This has been the case both in the past and the present.

    B. These two important topics have often had occasion to interact.

    C. This course will examine historical episodes in order to explore the various interactions that science and religion have had.

II. It is important, first of all, to define the basic terms and parameters of this study.

    A. This course focuses on the interactions of science and religion in the Latin West and its direct descendants (Western Europe and North America).

        1. This choice is based on the fact that not only modern science but most listeners (North Americans) are products most directly of the Latin West; thus, this domain presents both the most significant and the most relevant examples.

        2. Consequently, the religion discussed here is predominantly Western Christianity.

    B. The approach and content of this course are predominantly historical but also, to some extent, philosophical.

1. Many issues are long-lived; thus, there is an attempt to link historical episodes with their modern-day equivalents.
2. The emphasis is on scientific and theological *knowledge*; therefore, ethical issues are not treated.

C. Definitions of science and religion can skew our study if they are too rigid or drawn too naïvely from modern experience. Modern experience may not "map out" on the historical past.
   1. What counts as science (or religion) is, to a considerable extent, determined by the historical context; its definition is not rigidly fixed.
   2. Some broad, common definitions are useful, if we keep them flexible enough to grow under the influence of historical studies.

D. *Science*, in common parlance, is both a body of knowledge claims and a practice; it deals with the knowledge and study of the *natural* world.

E. *Religion* is difficult to define neatly; more useful and more precise terms are *religious practice*, *theology*, and *faith*.
   1. *Religious practice* can be defined as the observances and practices that flow from a religious commitment (attendance at church, works of charity, moral self-discipline, and so on).
   2. *Theology* is "a rational discourse about God"; that is, it is the intellectual and methodical study of God and the spiritual world and God's attributes, actions, and relationship to creation.
   3. Like science, theology is both a body of knowledge claims and a practice of generating them.
   4. *Faith* is a method (through belief or suspended disbelief) of arriving at some knowledge claim, for example, "that God exists."
   5. These three concepts are interconnected, but individuals combine them in different ways and proportions.

F. A useful pair of terms is *faith* and *reason*—both are methods of arriving at knowledge claims but by different routes.
   1. It is sometimes claimed that religion works by faith and science by reason and that this is the basis of their distinction; however, this claim is too sloppy.

2. Science must often depend on faith statements even though it uses reason extensively; likewise, theology relies on the exercise of reason.
3. Science and theology share considerable commonality and are (more rigorously speaking) the domains to be compared in this course.

III. Various models of the science-religion interaction have been proposed.

    A. The most common is the warfare model; this will be dealt with at length in Lecture Two.

    B. Another model is the separate realms model. It argues that science and religion address different domains, and by consequence, any conflict is a result of boundary transgressions.

        1. But this model relies upon *a priori*, modern, and sometimes idiosyncratic definitions of science and religion.

        2. Christian theology *does* make specific claims about the natural world, for example, that the world is not eternal.

        3. Likewise, science makes claims about the natural world that have direct bearing on theological claims.

        4. Trying to erect fences between science and religion is reactionary and, ultimately, *normative*. Historical inquiry cannot be normative; it has to be descriptive, analytical, and explanatory.

    C. Various forms of the *complexity thesis* have been proposed using such terms as *translation, appropriation, assimilation,* and *cross-fertilization*. This model relies on contextualized case studies to illustrate the diverse and complex interactions of science and religion.

Essential Reading:

John Hedley Brooke, *Science and Religion: Some Historical Perspectives*, pp. 1–33.

Margaret Osler, "Science and Religion in Early Modern Europe," *History of Science* 36 (1998): 91–113.

Supplementary Reading:

Stephen J. Gould, *Rocks of Ages: Science and Religion in the Fullness of Life*.

Questions to Consider:

1. Take some time to consider the bases of your own knowledge. How do you know what you know (about scientific ideas or religious ones)? At what point are you personally comfortable with making an assumption of truth (a faith leap) to create a foundation for your thought and beliefs? Can this be justified logically? Does it matter? Should it?

2. Identify and analyze your own thoughts about science and religion as you begin this course. What do you think their relationship has been? What is the source for your perceptions?

Lecture One—Transcript
Science and Religion

Science and religion: together they comprise two of the most important and wide-ranging influences on human civilization. When we survey the broad sweep of history, the impact of these two features of human civilization is everywhere apparent. A glance at the daily newspaper will convince you—that is, if you need convincing—that the two, both of them, continue to be important influences on our daily world, both for good and for ill. Their impact is everywhere. We can't escape either one.

Even the most avowedly nonreligious person can't elude the daily influence of religion in their lives in terms as obvious as current events, vocabulary, or the very ways we conceptualize the world. Likewise, even the scientifically untrained or uninterested can scarcely draw a breath without coming in contact with science or with one of its technological products. So even those who think that they are little concerned with either science or religion or both are really just deluding themselves like ostriches with their heads stuck in the sand.

Given the importance of these two subjects, it's not surprising that, down through the ages, they have had considerable chance to interact. So we are faced naturally with a simple question: what is the nature of that interaction? How have science and religion, that have independently so powerfully influenced human civilization, impacted each other? This course intends to examine just that question.

Over the next 12 lectures, we are going to explore several historical episodes that provide insights upon the varied interactions between science and religion. Of course, 12 lectures are very few. We can do little more than hit some of the high points of the science-religion interaction, but we're going to endeavor to fill out a broad view of the science-religion landscape and call into question some very common assumptions about it and, I hope along the way, correct some prevalent historical errors about the topic.

To get started, Aristotle advises us that we should begin any serious investigation by defining our terms. In my experience, I found it's always a good idea to listen to what Aristotle has to say, so let's heed his advice. We will first define the scope of this course and then see what we can do with those very slippery words, "science" and "religion."

There are many religions in the world, of course. And one could ask interesting questions about the relationship of any one of them with science. But this course is going to focus on the science-religion interactions specifically in the Latin West. What do I mean by the Latin West? What I mean are the lands that were once the Latin-speaking parts of the Roman Empire and its successors. In other words, predominantly Western Europe and the Mediterranean. In the sense I am using the term, I am also including one important offspring of European culture—that is, North America.

We can't cover everything in 12 lectures, but there are two more important justifications for this choice. The first is that modern science is predominantly a product of the Latin West. Therefore, if we want to draw meaningful connections between historical events and modern-day concerns, it seems most reasonable that we should choose to look at the culture that's most directly the progenitor of our own. Second, most of the listeners to this course, regardless of their religious affiliation or lack thereof, or of their historic ethnic origins, will be North Americans, and thus, by that very fact, immersed in a public and intellectual culture which is Western European in origin and character. Therefore, this Western European focus seems to make sense in terms of relevance.

This cultural focus immediately has one good advantage. It helps us define the religion upon which we will focus, namely Christianity, the dominant religion of European and New World culture. Having said this, we can now more rigorously define the scope of this course. It is the study of the interactions of Christianity with science in the Western tradition. Of course, there are many extremely interesting and enlightening episodes in religion-science interactions in Islam and in Judaism. But unfortunately, we can't cover them in this course.

There exists, I should point out, sufficient diversity within the Christian tradition anyway, particularly after the 16th-century Reformation and after the 19th-century explosion of North American splinter sects. So we are going to have our hands quite full just dealing with diversity within Christianity.

After examining definitions and some historical models for the science-religion interaction, we are then going to follow a mostly chronological sequence to examine some illustrative episodes. Some of these are going to be familiar to everybody, like the Galileo affair or the continuing fallout over issues of evolution, but there are others that will be less well known, for example, the issues regarding miracles and spirit interactions in the world, biblical interpretations, and medieval naturalism.

One thing there's already plenty of out there in discussions of science and religion is self-serving rhetoric as well as polemics and gross oversimplifications. Part of our job is to get beyond all of those, to achieve a well-grounded and, most of all, properly contextualized view of what really happened and why. So we want to untangle the real issues in play. And as we see, some of these issues are intricately philosophical and intellectual. Some of them are really going to bend your mind to get your brains around them. At other times, these issues will be political or social and sometimes just personal. What's certain is that the real stories are almost invariably much more interesting than the rhetorical polemical versions, even if the real stories are less useful in the end for bashing people over the head. Finally, in my last comment about the course, this is a course predominantly about scientific and theological knowledge. Therefore, I am not going to treat issues relating to ethics; that would certainly be a course on its own.

Now let's get to the difficult task: defining what we mean by science and religion. Here, frankly, we are stuck between a rock and a hard place. On the one hand, we need some precision in our terms so that we are sure that our discussions don't slip out from beneath us, owing to subtle shifts in our definitions or unclear terminology. Indeed, many of the misunderstandings between science-religion and their interactions, both historically and at the present day, stem from the sloppiness with which terms are bandied about. Often they are used more as rallying posts than as explanatory terminology. We want explanatory terminology.

But on the other hand, we also have to realize that any of the definitions that we give have a historically contingent component. That's a fancy way of saying that nobody, except maybe for some philosophers and lexicologists, actually start by making definitions and then classify things in the world according to the definitions they've just made. Rather, the real things exist first and then the definitions are wrapped around them with more or less neatness.

For example, let's take the astronomer Johannes Kepler. What he was doing at the turn of the 17th century was certainly scientific to him, but it might not fit our modern definitions of science, because those modern definitions were hammered out and rigorized in the 19th century for very specific purposes. So my point is that if we start out setting down definitions that are too rigid, too absolute, too modern, we automatically limit ourselves to speaking only about modern times. But this is a history course; we can't limit ourselves just to modern times.

If we start with definitions distinguishing science clearly from religion, which might probably seem reasonable enough to most people today, we start out simply enough on the wrong foot. Let me give you an example. A moment ago I mentioned Johannes Kepler, one of the most important astronomers and mathematicians of the early 17th century. He is cited in every elementary physics text as the discoverer of important laws of planetary motion, for example, that the planets orbit the sun in elliptical orbits with the sun at one focus of the ellipse. We can clearly recognize what we call science in Kepler's work. But Kepler was also explicit in saying that his motivation for uncovering the laws of nature was to give glory to their creator.

At one point he writes, "God is praised through my work in astronomy." Thus, was Kepler's motivation scientific or religious? Was he more involved in science or religion? The answer to those questions is simply that they are poorly phrased questions, poorly phrased because they illegitimately transfer our own definitions and boundaries from the 20th and 19th century back to Kepler's 17th century. For Kepler, a clear distinction between science and religion, which seems so obvious to us today, so unquestionable, simply didn't exist as such. And Kepler is not some oddball exception. The same could be said of Isaac Newton, for example, or any of their contemporaries or predecessors.

If you're interested in more examples of this sort, I will take this opportunity to direct you to my longer course on the history of science to 1700, which documents the close relationship, in fact, the inseparability of scientific and religious issues throughout the period that it covers. In this course, we are going to look at illustrative episodes in more detail and tease out the meanings to them. But let me get back to definitions. I must stress that part of our task here is to understand what was actually meant by science or religion in the past. And we can only do that by looking at things as they really existed. We are going to set ourselves up to fail if we create categories first and carry them back with us to the past. That would be "baggage" that we carry with us.

We find ourselves having to navigate between two extremes: no definition at all and too much definition. I suggest that the compromise solution is to start with the broadest definitions that are familiar to us that we can come to now, and then remember to leave ourselves open to amend, expand, alter, mutate those definitions as we go.

Let's start now with science. In common parlance, science actually has two distinct meanings. First, it is a body of knowledge claims. What do I mean by knowledge claims? I just mean a body of statements that are held or claimed to be true or probably true. Besides a body of knowledge claims, however, science is also a practice. The first definition is older because science, our English word "science," comes from the Latin *scientia*, which just means knowledge.

Since the 19th century, however, science has meant a specific kind of knowledge, namely, natural knowledge—that is, knowledge about the natural world. And we can rattle off a list of the various sciences with which we are familiar: botany, biology, astronomy, chemistry, and so forth. But besides this body of knowledge claims, science is also a practice. And by that I mean a set of methods for gaining, assessing, and augmenting the sum total of knowledge claims that science holds.

For example, say we are listening to the evening news one night, and we hear some kind of study that's just being reported. There is something wrong with it to our minds, and we say, "Oh well, that's not scientific." What do we mean by that? We mean that some standard agreed-upon rules of method, whether observation, testing, control, experiment, logical analysis, whatever it might be, has not been followed. So science has these two distinct meanings: body of knowledge claims and a practice for acquiring them.

Now, religion—here, clearly, we are in somewhat deeper waters. But the restriction of this course to Christianity means that we can avoid one really horrible question, that is, the philosophical and legal question of what constitutes a religion. Instead, we can just say, "Christianity is a religion" and move on. There are, however, three terms that describe different aspects of Christian religion. And these three terms I want to introduce because they are more precise than the sort of catch-all term "religion." They are going to make our discussions a little bit more precise—actually, I hope, a lot more precise.

The three that I have in mind are first, "religious practice;" two, "theology;" and three, "faith." Let's look at each one and give a definition of each in turn. First, religious practice. That can be defined as the observances and actions that flow from a religious commitment, for example, attending church, giving alms, praying, fasting at particular periods, moral self-discipline, and so forth; you can add to the list. Theology is the intellectual, methodical study of God, the spiritual world, God's attributes, actions, and relationship to creation. Like science, theology is composed of two parts: A set of knowledge claims (for example, Christ has a dual nature) and a practice for generating these knowledge claims. The third term, faith, is a method of arriving at knowledge claims. The method is by simple belief, by assumption, or suspended disbelief.

Now that we've defined these three, how are the three actually related? You can work out a good deal of this on your own I think. Think about it for a while. Think about people you know. Think about yourself. Think about examples. And try to tease out the three different facets of religion in those people or those examples. Let me give you a couple of examples that came to my mind. One, we could have two individuals, both of whom display a high level of religious practice. One could have a highly developed theological sense and rely very little on faith. The other one, however, could have a very large investment in faith and very little theology. It's possible even to simultaneously be an atheist and a theologian. All that would mean is that you use the methods of theology to generate a number of statements, but without actually investing those statements with personal belief. So that's possible as well.

I should also say that faith need not mark out people that we would term "religious." The example is that to be an atheist requires a great leap of faith, that is, to assent to the unprovable statement, the unprovable premise that no God exists. So, in fact, a theist and an atheist are both people of faith, they are both believers. It just happens that one belief is negative, and the other one is affirmative.

There are probably as many permutations and combinations of these three within a religious person as there are people. I will let you think about that a little further on your own. After having said this, it seems to me that when we are talking about science and religion, what we are really talking about most of the time is science and theology. There is little point, for example, in talking about, say, science and religious belief or religious practice because there's not enough similarity between the two to make any kind of comparisons meaningful. But science and theology share a lot in common. Both are bodies of knowledge claims and practices. And the practices are not entirely similar, but they do have things that can be compared. They form a pair that's very well suited for comparison.

Let's go a little deeper here. The content of both science and religion is made up of statements and claims about the way things are; science, about the way things are predominantly, but not entirely, in the natural world; theology predominantly, but not entirely, about the way things are in the spiritual world. Examination of their practices is really very revealing. We've already encountered faith as a method of generating statements or claims. But let's name another method, namely, reason. How do faith and reason relate to one another? That's a very important question, and really it lies at the core of a great deal of what we usually refer to as the science-religion interaction; often it's really a faith-reason kind of interaction instead.

How do faith and reason relate to one another? Well that's been a fundamental question for millennia. I am going to devote lecture three almost entirely to that question. But for now, we need to tease out just some starting point for our discussions, so a short answer will be enough. Faith and reason are both methods for generating a knowledge claim. Faith functions by means of belief. A premise is stated and believed true, generally on the basis of some sort of authority. In short, it's assumed true.

Christianity maintains a body of such statements that are handed down within its tradition. Now different Christians may argue about exactly what those faith statements are, but there's a considerable amount of agreement. For example, the collection of Nicaean Creed at the beginning of the 4th century. It includes, for example, the faith statement, "I believe in one God." Creed, by the way, derives from the Latin word *credo*, "I believe," a word that is repeated at the beginning of every section of the Nicaean Creed. The point is that the exercise of faith provides a body of knowledge claims— remember, knowledge claims being a set of statements that are claimed to be true or probably true.

The exercise of reason, on the other hand, takes us from premises to conclusions by the means of argument and logic. As a method, it's obviously more complicated and open to greater analysis than is faith. But it leads to a similar product—a collection of knowledge claims. Now to the key point. In discussing science and religion, it's sometimes claimed that science operates by means of reason and religion by faith, and that this difference of method is the basis of their distinction. But think about it for a little while; you will see that this is a false idea.

Traditional Christian theology does not operate by faith alone. At every moment, it relies upon logical argument, deduction, and reason. The works of medieval theologians for example are masterpieces of logical analysis and rational argument. I like to point out that the principle, the logical principle known as Ockham's Razor, which is often used and sometimes abused in modern scientific discussions, is actually named after William of Ockham, a 14th-century Franciscan theologian.

It may be that the medieval theologians' rational arguments began from, or are bounded by, certain statements held by faith. But in fact, again if you think about it, scientific arguments are really not that different. Science as we know it incorporates a substantial number of faith statements simply in order to operate. While the specifics of scientific study and reasoning generally stem from empirical evidence, which is one of the defining characteristics of science, there also exist many implicit assumptions. For example, most natural scientists make the leap of faith—a leap that's been assailed recently by some modern critics—that they are studying something that's real, that the natural world, the physical world, actually exists, that it has an independent existence outside of ourselves.

A related assumption is that the world is uniform in the sense that its behavior is regular and law-like. Likewise, assumptions have to be made about sense perception. We have to assume that our senses are giving us in some way—whether we are looking directly at a natural object or reading an instrument or a scale or looking through a telescope—we have to assume that our senses are giving us some kind of authentic, reliable information. And we have to rely on our subsequent ability to register and interpret those sensations correctly. These are all statements that cannot be proven true. Of course without such assumptions, it would be futile, for example, to bother trying to determine natural laws if we believe that they changed every few minutes.

But recognizing such implicit assumptions, which are ultimately expressions of faith, shouldn't lead us to diminish the status or the ability of science to tell us about our world one wit. Instead it shows that the basis of our knowledge claims about the world are invariably grounded upon certain assumptions that are outside the realm of reason. This does not imply that they are unreasonable; notice, only—and this is the important point—it shows us that the exercise of human reason has its limits. We have to accommodate ourselves to positing some ground level assumptions with which we are comfortable that rest ultimately upon beliefs, assumptions, leaps of faith. Once we do that, then we can progress.

The point here is by no means to undermine science, either as a body of knowledge claims or as a practice, but rather to show the inadequacy of making too facile a separation between science and theology based on their deployment of faith versus reason. Both of them employ both. Good theology and good science are methodologically quite similar, even if the things that they are making claims about are often, but not always, quite different.

Let's move from philosophy to history and look at historical claims about the interactions of science and religion. Many models for the interaction between science and religion have been proposed over time. Probably the most common of all these is the conflict or "warfare model." The model states, as you can tell from the title, that science and religion, or scientists and religionists, form two separate and warring camps. This model is so prevalent and provides such an interesting example of how commonly held beliefs come to be developed and maintained that I've decided to devote an entire lecture to it. That will be our next lecture, lecture number two. For right now, I will just mention its existence and move on.

Another model is what's called the "separate realms model." This states that science and religion operate in fundamentally different realms of knowledge and activity. In one version—not all versions, but in one version—science deals with the physical world, while religion deals with morals and ethics. Another version of this was proposed by the paleontologist and popular writer, Stephen Jay Gould, and called by him NOMA, for non-overlapping magisteria, that is to say, that science and religion have their own independent autonomous separate spheres of authority.

A consequence of this model is that any time a conflict appears between science and religion, it must be the result of a border transgression. There is something in this formulation of the separate realms model that appeals to our innate sense of fairness and professionalism. Still, there are serious critiques of it to be made. First, it's clearly a post-conflict model. It assumes that, in its absence, things are going to run into conflict. It's an attempt to play the referee and find agreeable borders. It's in a sense saying, "All right children, play nice, and stay within the yards I've marked out for you." As a result, it really doesn't have very much value to the historian because the boundaries that it sets forth are not trans-historical. They are the result of history.

Thus, it can't help us understand the historical record. It would be anachronistic to apply it to situations where the boundaries were different. Remember, for example, the Kepler instance I mentioned. And it runs the risk of making us arrogant because we're tempted, maybe even encouraged, to use it as a ruler by which to measure up historical incidence. When they don't measure up, we tut-tut and wag our finger at some presumed border transgression without acknowledging that the borders have actually shifted considerably.

The Latin word for ruler or carpenter square, *norma*, gives us a word to describe this kind of model. It is a normative model. It tells us how things ought to be, that is, it sets down a pattern or a norm, but of course, a norm that has been arrived at by a particular person at a particular time and place. Historians eschew the normative. Our job is to be descriptive, interpretative, and explanatory. The normative— well, the normative we leave to philosophers, moralists, umpires, and other know-it-alls.

As we progress through this course, we should instead pay attention to the ever-shifting and ever-fuzzy borders of science and religion, and we will see again that in the past, they don't lie where we expect them to. Some of the most interesting and most productive interactions occurred from what we might call "crossovers," border transgressions—the borrowing of terms, methods, and ideas from one realm into another. Indeed, historians of science recently have taken to talking up appropriations and translations between science and religion to describe the regular exchange and readaptation of materials between science and theology, typical of periods before the 19th century.

But there's another critique of the separate realms model to be made. Simply, Christianity does make claims about the natural world—for example, that the world is not eternal. It's a dogma of Christianity. Such claims do overlap with the claims of natural science. Likewise, some scientific work, either directly or indirectly, makes claims that overlap with theology. The assertion made by some writers that religion deals only with morals or ethics (or should) virtually identifies these authors as modern English liberal Protestants, that is to say, products of a particular historical development.

Traditional Christianity contains knowledge claims about the way things are in the natural world. Historians of science nowadays generally adopt some version of what's called the complexity thesis. It's not as neat or as simple as the conflict or separate realms model, but it has the advantage of being historically more accurate. Namely, there is no one simple description to the science-religion issue. There have certainly been episodes that can be described as conflicts, but having said that, as historians, we need to go further to analyze and specify what's really going on, to learn what it can tell us about the thoughts and ideas that informed each episode.

Likewise, there have been points of harmony or collaboration, and these too need to be examined for what they tell us and provide a contrast to the common assumptions of conflict. On a larger scale, this is going to teach us something about the familiar, the here and now, that the here and now is neither inevitable or the only way that things can be. This in fact, it seems to me, is one of the fundamental reasons for studying history. It's not to be normative, that is, for us to go around telling our predecessors what they should have been. Instead, it's rather to give them the chance to explain to us what we might have been and yet could be.

Lecture Two
The Warfare Thesis

Scope:

In this lecture, we examine one formulation of the historical relationship between science and religion—the *warfare* or *conflict thesis*. Loudly advanced in the late 19th century by two men—John William Draper and Andrew Dickson White—it has continued strong in popular thought down to the present day. We will examine how this formulation rests on very shaky (and sometimes fabricated) foundations and was contrived largely for quite specific political, professional, and racist purposes. One value of this examination is to create a catalogue of methodological errors and fallacies for all readers of history to be on guard against. Serious modern historians of science have unanimously dismissed the warfare model as an adequate historical description.

Outline

I. The model for the interactions of science and religion most commonly encountered in popular literature and common belief is the *warfare* or *conflict thesis*.

   A. The conflict or warfare thesis maintains that throughout history, religion and science have been opposed and inimical. Religion has stymied the advance of science.

   B. No serious historians of science or of the science-religion issue today maintain the warfare thesis.

   C. It is crucial to examine the origins of common beliefs, such as this one, and the solidity of their foundations.

   1. The origins of the warfare thesis lie in the late 19th century, specifically in the work of two men—John William Draper and Andrew Dickson White.

   2. These men had specific political purposes in mind when arguing their case, and the historical foundations of their work are unreliable.

II. John William Draper (1811–1882), son of an English Methodist minister, was a chemist, physician, and first president of the American Chemical Society, who wrote *A History of the Conflict between Religion and Science* in 1874.

   A. The book was commissioned by a popular science publisher for the International Scientific Series. It outsold every other title in this extensive series, went through 50 printings and 10 translations, and remains readily available.

   B. The book is not good history; historical "facts" are confected, and causes and chronologies are twisted to the author's purpose.

   C. The text is actually one long, vitriolic, anti-Catholic diatribe.
      1. Draper blames the Catholic Church for almost everything bad in Western history (including preventing the "proper" expansion of the human population).
      2. Part of Draper's ire results from the First Vatican Council's then-recent declarations, particularly against abuses of rationalism, namely, the council's assertion that there are revealed truths that are not accessible to unaided reason, that is, to rational (scientific) inquiry.
      3. Much of Draper's text exemplifies the widespread Anglo-American anti-Catholicism and racism of the period—particularly opposition to new (Catholic) immigrants in America.
      4. At the same time, Protestantism is seen as the twin sister of modern science, and when Protestants cause problems, it is either on account of "misunderstandings" or because they are incompletely "emancipated" from Catholicism.

   D. Although Draper's work is easy to dismiss as cranky and ahistorical, his theme and many of his anecdotes have entered the common consciousness, where they have remained hard to remove.

III. A more sustained, and seemingly more historical, presentation of the warfare thesis appeared in a series of publications by Andrew Dickson White.

   A. White first treated the subject in 1869, published a longer version (*The Warfare of Science*) in 1876, and eventually put out a ponderous two-volume work, *A History of the Warfare of Science with Theology in Christendom*, in 1896.

1. White was a historian at the University of Michigan and, later, the first president of Cornell University.
2. White's books, although still melodramatic in tone to modern tastes, did not share the rabidity of Draper and did not sell as well. But their apparent historical documentation gave them greater influence.
3. White's interest was provoked by criticism he received for establishing Cornell without religious affiliation.

B. Despite appearances, White's arguments are scarcely better than Draper's.
1. White uses fallacious arguments and suspect or bogus sources.
2. His methodological errors are collectivism (the unwarrantable extension of an individual's views to represent that of some larger group of which he is a part), a lack of critical judgment about sources, argument by ridicule and assertion, failure to check primary sources, and quoting selectively and out of context.
3. White popularized the baseless notions that before Columbus and Magellan, the world was thought to be flat and that the Earth's sphericity was officially opposed by the Church.
4. He is also responsible for the equally fallacious notion that the Church forbade human dissection.
5. The notion—eternally repopularized by Hollywood—that the medieval Church condemned all science as devilry runs throughout White; this view is likewise baseless.

IV. These works are of interest in terms of their 19th-century context but have no general historical value for the science-religion issue.

A. Besides poor scholarship, these books rely on a central and fallacious assumption: that scientists and theologians formed two separate camps throughout history and that theologians imposed their will on scientists.
1. These categories are modern—rigorized only in the 19th century.
2. The pre-modern thinkers retroactively called *scientists* themselves believed that theology and religious texts were relevant to their work and vice versa.

3. Thus, religion was not an external imposition but a key part of the mental landscape of pre-modern natural philosophers.
4. Divisions between science and religion that might seem familiar today are *not* transhistorical.

B. Despite the shoddy character of these publications, they were (and continue to be) widely influential. Their influence stems in part from their success in creating a *myth for science as a religion*, embraced ever since by science advocates.

C. The historian's task now is to analyze specific episodes contextually, to fill out a comprehensive view of issues and interactions, without recourse to "sound bite" oversimplifications.

Essential Reading:

David C. Lindberg and Ronald L. Numbers, eds., *God and Nature: Historical Essays on the Encounter between Christianity and Science*, Introduction.

Brooke, *Science and Religion*, pp. 33–51.

Supplementary Reading:

Lindberg and Numbers, "Beyond War and Peace."

Questions to Consider:

1. Think about how erroneous notions in history arise and are passed down from generation to generation (for example, Columbus and a flat Earth, the constant warfare of science and religion, and so on). Is it possible to put these errors to rest? How would you go about it?

2. One possible excuse for Draper and White might be that the telling of history had a different purpose in the 19th century than now, namely, that it placed greater emphasis on instilling a "moral" than on being accurate. Critique this view and think about the "uses and abuses" of history then and now. What should we tolerate and not tolerate from historical treatments?

Lecture Two—Transcript
The Warfare Thesis

In the last lecture, we looked at some models for the interaction between science and religion. I concluded at that point with the suggestion that the interaction has been so complicated over time that we can't use any one blanket description; instead, I proposed the complexity thesis. But at that time, I also mentioned the conflict thesis as one of the most prevalent of the blanket descriptions for religion-science interactions, and in this lecture, we are going to look more closely at that conflict model.

It is a good idea, I think in general, to look at where our assumptions and preconceptions come from. One of the things I find very interesting about the conflict model is that it's been reinforced to equal degrees by people on both sides of this science-religion controversy. The strangely persistent issue of creationism and evolution that we hear something about almost every day now in the newspapers renews the perception of conflict. And scientists as well often make statements that are fairly aggressively antireligious. So the conflict model has these people constantly reinforcing it as well.

But one of the best things about history, to my mind, is that it gives us a sense of perspective—a perspective that often reveals how strange and atypical our times are in relation to the past. So given the widespread public acceptance of the conflict model, it comes as a surprise to many people to learn that no historians will support it. Let me be clear; the idea that scientific and religious camps have historically been separate and antagonistic is rejected by all modern historians of science. So let's explore its origins.

Why, when, and by whom was it proposed? How is it defended and how was it disseminated so widely? What's the evidence for it? Is there a particular context and reason for its formulation? And finally, how do we explain its long-term success? Now in history, we have to realize that it often proves quite difficult to answer questions of origins and causation with precision and certainty. But this is not the case with the warfare model of science and religion. Its origins are easy to pin down.

So I am going to begin with some simple declarative statements. One, the conflict model is a fabrication of the late 19th century. Two, its origins lie with two men, John William Draper and Andrew

Dixon White. Third, these men had specific political and social purposes when arguing their case. And fourth, most importantly, the historical foundations for their work are almost totally unreliable. Let's look more closely.

John William Draper was born in England in 1811, the son of an itinerant Methodist preacher. He immigrated to the United States in 1832 and received a medical degree from the University of Pennsylvania in 1836. In due course, he took up a position as a professor of chemistry, first at Hampden-Sydney College in Virginia and then at New York University. He was eventually also named the first president of the American Chemical Society. In the 1860s, he turned from his scientific work toward publishing on historical subjects including, in 1863, a book that was entitled *A History of the Intellectual Development of Europe.*

This publication manifested Draper's embrace of positivism, the positivism of August Comte, particularly his law of the three stages of human development. In brief, Comte had claimed that all human history progresses through three successive stages: the first being the theological and the lowest, then the metaphysical, and finally the highest stage, the positive stage or the scientific stage. Such a theory, as untenable as it's now seen to be, was sweet music—not to say sweet flattery—to the ears of 19th-century scientists. This was the period they were trying to professionalize their fields. This was the period in which the word "scientist" was coined for the first time. The industrial revolution was in full swing, and its products of science, technology, and manufacture were daily being felt more and more on a constant basis by ordinary people. Scientists themselves at this time were eager to create, define, and elevate their social position. So the positivism of Comte that put scientific thought at the top of the heap was a welcome boost for scientists.

Additionally, Draper loved the idea of immutable laws governing everything—not just science, but culture and history as well. As a result of Draper's historical writing, the most successful science popularizer in America, Edward L. Youmans, asked Draper to contribute a volume to his international scientific series. This series eventually contained more than 40 volumes, and by the time he asked Draper, it already contained books on several scientific topics which had been commissioned from leading scientists.

Draper's contribution, which was published in 1874, was a history of the conflict between religion and science. Its success was phenomenal. It outsold every other title in the series. It went through over 50 printings, was translated into 10 languages and even today, 130 years later, remains readily available. Draper's main sentiments are summed up in the first few pages, where he writes, "The history of science is a narrative of the conflict of two contending powers: the expansive force of human intellect and the compression arising from traditionary faith." With these references to expansion and compression, it sounds rather like Draper the chemist discussing gas laws. But in fact, he uncomplicatedly identifies expansion as science and compression as religion.

How does he support his contention of conflict? Unfortunately, with some of the worst historical writing you are ever likely to come across. Historical facts are confected, causes and chronologies twisted to the author's purpose. We find interpretations made merely by declaration. We find quotations violently taken out of context and instances, quite a few of them, where Draper claims a historical writer said something that's, in fact, 180 degrees away from what he actually claimed. Let me give you an example. At one point, Draper ridicules St. Augustine for saying that the sky is stretched flat over the earth like a skin. If we go look up St. Augustine, in fact that line does occur there, but it's a quotation that St. Augustine makes out of the psalms. Why does Augustine cite it? He uses it as an example of how biblical interpreters must be careful not to accept the surface text of scripture, since here, as St. Augustine notes, it obviously conflicts with established astronomical knowledge. Indeed, Draper declares that, "No one more than Augustine brought science and religion into antagonism." In a future lecture, we will see just how wrong that statement is.

Much of Draper's book is so ridiculous, so melodramatic, so rabid that it's hard for a knowledgeable person actually to read it without a wry smirk. In fact, I find when I am teaching science and religion to my students, I always want to give them some kind of points of discussion in terms of photocopies out of Draper's book, but I've never actually been able to find something I didn't think they'd laugh at.

But further, it's not just any religion that Draper assails. Draper's book is actually one long vitriolic rant specifically against Catholicism. Rather than the impartial account he promises readers in the introduction, Draper runs to sarcasm, ridicule, and absurdities. In fact, large sections of his text pass by without any discussion of science and religion issues in order to assail what he calls "the corruption of Christianity into Romanism," and quite literally, everything that is laid at the feet of the Catholic Church, which he claims to "have ever held a bitter mortal animosity towards all science." In fact, Draper may be the only person in history ever to blame the Catholic Church for the prevention of the expansion of human population.

How does he manage this? First, he asserts as a law—there's one of those laws that Draper loved so much—that the human population should double every 25 years. And then he claims that in the 500 years from 1066 to the Reformation, the population of England scarcely doubled. Thus he concludes Catholicism is to blame, partly on account of priestly celibacy, partly on account of insinuated clerical debaucheries that prevented legitimate proper marriages—you can tell he's a Victorian Englishman, right, because he thinks that you need a proper marriage for children, but let that pass—partly on account of excessive death from famine, disease, and lack of due medical care, all of which of course is the Pope's fault. I am not making this up.

By the way, perhaps he never did the math, but given his law of population and the starting population of England of two million that he provides, if it weren't for the supposed suppression of the population by the Vatican's policies, then the population of England in 1566 would have been about two trillion, or 350 times the current population of the planet. What could provoke such claims? Two things: First, Draper flies off the handle at several mentions of the first Vatican Council, which had been convened in 1870, just four years before his book came out. One of the things about it that got his goat apparently was the council's criticism of rationalism, namely, the belief that all knowledge and truth is immediately accessible to, and subject to, reason. The council instead affirmed that human reason, while powerful, is nonetheless limited in its extent, for there exists certain transcendent truths, for example, the triune nature of God that could not be revealed by unaided reason.

So Draper reprints some of the things that annoy him the most about Vatican I's dogmatic constitution at the back of his book. But the intensity of his response remains still a little hard to account for after you've read this. This is because Draper's tone is not entirely rational, but is partly emotional. That is, it is grounded in the fervent Anglo-American anti-Catholicism and racism of the late 19th century, particularly sparked by opposition to new Catholic immigrants to America. Indeed, we can remark with just a smirk that he doesn't seem to have noticed that the mid-19th-century doubling of the American population, at what he calls "the prescribed rate," and which he uses to prove the superiority of new Protestant America to Catholic Old Europe, was in fact due in significant part to Irish immigration.

Anyway, Draper calls Protestantism the twin sister of science. Any conflicts came only from misunderstandings or from Protestants being—and this is his term—"incompletely emancipated from Catholic-type thinking." What I find particularly odd is his adulation of Islam, which he actually calls the "Southern Reformation." Part of this comes from his unexplained contempt for the doctrine of the Trinity, for which he invents an Egyptian origin. But another part of it comes from his implicit belief that probably anything would be better than Catholicism. Although Draper's book was popular, some people apparently found this topic a little bit humorous as well because, in the 1870s after the book was published, a cartoon came out in New York that showed Draper dressed in a turban and pointed shoes, waiving a scimitar engraved with the name of his book in front of the pope, who held a scroll saying, "Infallibility." Underneath is a poem that goes in part like this: "Now, by the holy prophet's beard, the pain in Draper cries, and flourishes his scimitar before St. Peter's eyes. 'Tis I who am infallible, as all the world doth know. By science bright and Islam's might, 'tis I that tell thee so."

Draper's support of American anti-Catholicism and anti-immigrant sentiment is certainly one of the reasons his book found such a wide readership. But it also found a public steeped in the ideas of scientific progress, eager for the new science, and ready to benefit from its promises—promises which are made abundantly throughout Draper's book. It was also a time of considerable discussion of science and religion anyway because it falls in the aftermath of Darwinian evolution. But we will postpone that particular discussion to a later lecture.

While Draper's work is easy to dismiss as cranky and ahistorical, a more sustained and seemingly more historical presentation of the warfare thesis came out at about the same time from Andrew Dixon

White. Who was White? He was born in America in 1832 and raised as an Episcopalian. Unlike Draper, he was actually a historian, first at the University of Michigan, then he became the first president of Cornell University and then the president of the American Historical Association. He first treated the subject in 1869. In 1876, he published a version entitled *The Warfare of Science*, and he went on a lecture tour giving talks about this issue. These short publications grew into a ponderous two-volume work entitled *A History of the Warfare of Science with Theology in Christendom*, published in 1896.

White's books are still melodramatic in tone to modern readers, modern tastes, but they don't share Draper's rabidity. Perhaps for this reason and for the reason they weren't hawked by a big popularizer like Youmans, they didn't sell as well. Nonetheless, as a result of the copious footnotes that they contained, they seemed to be more reliable and so, in effect, had a greater impact certainly on the historical community, if not the popular community.

Why was White interested in the subject? He was driven to it by criticism he received as president of Cornell University, one of the first educational institutions in America that had been established without religious affiliation and which embraced an entirely secular program of study. Thus, White's strategy was to reply to his critics by trying to use history to show, as he said, "Interference with science in the supposed interest of religion has resulted in the direst evils, both to religion and science, and invariably so." The book is, in short, a projection of his experience with Cornell onto history.

Let's take a few minutes to examine some of his arguments. Unfortunately, when examined for historical accuracy, his arguments, even though footnoted, are not much better than Draper's. What I hope to do here is not only to criticize White—criticizing White is unnecessary at this point—but also to fill out a catalogue of common historical errors that you might want to keep in mind whenever you are reading any kind of book or treatment of history.

Let's start with a simple and a notorious example: the idea that before Columbus, people thought that the world was flat. In fact, it is Draper and White specifically, both of them, who bear most of the blame for popularizing this baseless view to the extent that nowadays 80 percent of school teachers still foist this upon poor innocent schoolchildren. The fact is that of course the sphericity of the earth was well established by the 5th century B.C. by the Greeks and a good measure of its circumference made by the 3rd century B.C. And these facts were never forgotten in learned Western culture.

Ancient knowledge on this score was much more than what White calls "vague germ ideas." How did White and Draper get things so wrong? First, what they did was to dig up virtually the only two flat-earthers from late antiquity. Lactantius in the 3rd century and the extraordinarily obscure Cosmas Indicopleustes, a merchant of the 6th century. Then they made these two unimportant characters fill in for the entirety of intellectuals for a thousand years. Are they really representative? Not at all. The text of Cosmas in fact was not even known in the Middle Ages; it was discovered only in the 18th century and published then.

The historical fault here I want you to take home as a lesson is called "collectivism," and that is the unwarrantable extension of an individual's views to represent the views of a larger group of which he is considered a part. Thus, White and Draper, too—whom White seems to have copied—pick Lactantius and Cosmas as the paradigms and extend their view to represent all church writers, which involves ignoring everybody else. We could do the same thing today of course. If we wanted to say something about what Americans think, we'd go and pick a publication out of the Flat Earth Society located in California and conclude from it that Americans think the world is flat.

White then tells of a brave Columbus who fought mightily for the revolutionary notion of the earth's sphericity. And here he helps us out, damning himself, with a footnote that reads, "W. Irving, *Life of Columbus*." Yes indeed, this is Washington Irving of Rip Van Winkle in *Headless Horseman* fame who wrote a fictionalized account of Columbus in 1838. Yet White uses it as a historical source. This is an error of critical judgment. It's the same as if we used *The Da Vinci Code* as if it contained some historical realities. In fact, while White, echoing Irving, tells of a daring Columbus before an ignorant, sneering mob of clerics at the University of Salamanca, the real debate was far different. The debate at Salamanca was about the size of the earth, not its shape. Columbus was rightly criticized for thinking the earth vastly too small, by about the width of the Pacific Ocean—so about a third. The fear was that Columbus could never hold enough provisions to sail as far as Asia, not that he'd fall off the edge.

White then goes on to ridicule the papal role in settling disputes between Spain and Portugal over possessions in the New World. He says, "In 1493, Pope Alexander VI issues a bull laying down a line of demarcation upon the earth as a flat disc. This was hailed as an exercise of divinely illuminated power within the church." White claims that the document then "soon passed into the catalog of ludicrous errors" because, of course, one could get to the west side of the line by sailing east the long way around. However, let's go back and look at the original source. The papal bull, *Inter Cetera*, specifically says that the line goes, "From Arctic pole to Antarctic pole," and of course, you can't have poles unless you have a globe. So here is White's, as an example of a failure to check sources.

Another common fallacy that White broadcast and which is still popular today—very common, I have to fight against this in students all the time—was that the church forbade human dissection. It's true that there was a strong taboo against cutting open the human body among the ancient Romans, and this is why the 2nd-century physician, Galen, dissected instead monkeys and dogs and then transferred his anatomical discoveries by analogy to human beings. And this distaste endured for some time, but never was human dissection forbidden by Christian authorities. In fact, well before the end of the Middle Ages, attendance at a specific number of human dissections was a required part of medical education.

To carry his point, White writes the following, "St. Augustine"— poor Augustine, he gets such a bad rap from these folk—"in his great treatise on the City of God, which remains today one of the treasures of the church, speaks with bitterness of 'medical men who are called anatomists who, with a cruel zeal for science, have dissected the bodies of the dead and sometimes of sick persons who have died under their knives and inhumanely pried into the secrets of the human body to learn the nature of disease and its exact seat and how it might be cured.'" For White, this is a condemnation of anatomy.

But let's turn to the original text. St. Augustine, *De civitate Dei,* Book 22, Chapter 24. I will even quote from the same translation that White did, except what I am going to do is I am going to read a little bit before and a little bit after. Bear with me; it's a slightly long quotation, but it's all important. Augustine writes:

> No part of the body has been created for the sake of utility which does not also contribute something to its beauty. And this would be all the more apparent if we knew more precisely how all its parts are connected and adapted to one

another. And were we not limited in our observations to what lies on the surface. For as to what is covered up and hidden from view, the intricate web of veins and nerves, the vital parts of all that lies under the skin, no one can discover it. For although [and here comes the part quoted by White] with a cruel zeal for science, some medical men who were called anatomists have dissected the bodies of the dead and sometimes even of sick persons who died under their knives and have inhumanly pried into the secrets of the human body to learn the nature of disease in its exact seat and how it might be cured, [notice White stops here] yet, those relations of which I speak and which form the concord or as the Greeks call it, the harmony of the whole body outside and in as some musical instrument, no one has yet been able to discover because no one has yet been audacious enough to seek for them. But if these were known, then even the inward parts of the human body, which seem to have no beauty, would so delight us with their exquisite fitness as to afford a profounder satisfaction to the mind than the obvious beauty that gratifies the eye.

What Augustine is actually saying is that even the yucky guts of corpses are beautiful in their form and function and proclaim the wisdom of God, their creator. Only an abusively selective quotation could possibly turn this text into a prohibition against dissection. So here we have another historical fault: selective quotation out of context.

We have time for one more example. White tells of the 13th-century Franciscan, Roger Bacon, how he was in prison for science studies. Actually, though, Bacon's three major works were written at the request of Pope Clement IV, and if Bacon was actually imprisoned, it's not entirely certain—the sources are unclear—it was probably for writing books without the explicit permission of the Vicar General. In White's account, Bacon's experiments resulted in pandemonium, "Everywhere were priests, fellows, and students rushing about, their garments streaming in the wind, and everywhere resounded the cry 'down with the conjurer.'" One might be rude enough to ask exactly what his source is for this. But the first linkage of Bacon to sorcery actually comes in a 16th-century play, 300 years after Bacon.

I will remark at this point only that the condemnation of science as demonic, which is endlessly repeated in bad Hollywood productions, is not a feature in the Middle Ages. But we will come back to talk about demons in our fourth lecture. At any rate, White then shifts gears immediately and remarks, "In 1868 and 1869, sixty thousand children died in England and Wales of Scarlet Fever. Had not Bacon been hindered, we should have had in our hands by this time the means to save two-thirds of these victims, and the same is true of typhoid, typhus, and so forth." Do I really have to explain what's wrong with that? It's a bald emotional assertion based on nothing. It's totally worthless.

The only thing I wonder about is why do you suppose White only saved two-thirds of the poor babes? Maybe he thought that all of them was excessively optimistic and half not quite enough, so he took something in the middle. As you can see, refuting White is like shooting fish in a barrel. With his combination of bad sources, argument by assertion, quoting out of context, collectivism, and general reliance on exclamation rather than evidence and argument, White's is not a book to be taken seriously. Its real value is as a relic of its particular time and place, and as a museum of how not to write history.

I often wonder—he should have known better. Why did he write a book like this? It's so bad. And the best I can come up with is that perhaps he thought that his case was so important he had to argue like a lawyer, and that is less concerned about truth than about winning the case. That's the only way I can explain it.

There is a fundamental flaw that I haven't mentioned with the conflict thesis. It's the fallacious assumption that scientists and theologians formed two separate camps throughout history and that the theologians imposed their will on the scientists. But before the 19th century, scientific inquiry—better called natural philosophical inquiry at this time—was not carried out by a distinct professional class. Throughout the Middle Ages, natural philosophy was generally done in the context of theological speculation. People from before the 19th century, who we retrospectively call scientists, themselves believed that theology and religious texts, like the Bible, were relevant to their work. They would have reacted with puzzlement to the modern suggestion that they should have kept the two separate. They wouldn't have known what we were talking about. Thus religion was not an external imposition, but a key part of the mental landscape of premodern natural philosophers. There were simply not two camps.

But while we can look today with astonishment upon the shoddy character of Draper and White's writings, their books have had enormous impact, and we can't deny that. Much of this is due to their great success in creating a myth for science as a religion. Their myth of science as a religion is replete with battles and martyrdoms, saints and creeds. And as we know, or should know, myths are often much more powerful than historical realities. This myth was embraced by those who adulated science as a concept and as a culture, and it functioned as a means for identifying an identity for science and scientists, just at the time that they were hammering out this identity.

I say, with a little professional shame, that there were even historians of science that continue to support the views of Draper and White as late as the 1950s. Additionally, some scientists, particularly those of the crusading atheist variety, referred to them long after that. One egregious example is the cosmologist Carl Sagan, ironically enough another representative of White's Cornell University, who regurgitated sections of them seriously in his popular science program, *Cosmos*.

We have now explored not only the inherent faults, but also the contextual pressures and purposes for which these views were written a hundred years ago. It's now time to let them go. The historian's task is to analyze specific episodes contextually in order to fill out a comprehensive view of issues and interactions, without recourse to sound byte oversimplifications. In our next lecture, we are going to get on with it and examine ideas about faith, reason, and biblical interpretation as expounded by St. Augustine in the 5th century.

Lecture Three
Faith and Reason—Scripture and Nature

Scope:

In this lecture, we confront some basic conceptual and philosophical issues in the science-religion question: What are the legitimate *means* of acquiring sure knowledge, and what are *sources* from which we can obtain such knowledge? The answers invoke faith and reason as the means and "God's Two Books" (the Bible and the created world) as the sources. Here, we examine approaches to these means and sources in the Christian tradition, foundationally in St. Augustine's 5th-century writings and more recently in the important 1998 encyclical *Fides et ratio*.

Outline

I. Faith and reason are two means of obtaining knowledge statements; two sources of knowledge statements are the traditional "Two Books": the Book of Scripture and the Book of Nature.

II. St. Augustine (354–430) produced a profound synthesis between Greek philosophical thought and Christian belief, thus creating theological systems and methods foundational to Christianity.

   A. St. Augustine was born in North Africa to a Christian mother and pagan father. He rejected Christianity because its teachings seemed uncertain or illogical and the Bible seemed full of contradictions and nonsense.

   B. After study of Classical philosophers and travel in Italy, Augustine found an intellectual approach to Christianity (through Neo-Platonism) and biblical exegesis that satisfied him, and he eventually was baptized.

   C. St. Augustine made fundamental statements concerning our questions: the relationship of faith and reason and the correct methods of biblical interpretation.

      1. Reason and logical technique are necessary for theological inquiry. Augustine's early objections to Christianity were against intellectually primitive forms.

2. St. Augustine was following a scholarly tradition expressed by some earlier Christian writers, such as St. Clement of Alexandria.

III. St. Augustine argued for four points that not only became fundamental to Christian theology but are key to the science-religion interaction.

  A. First is the doctrine of the unity of truth.

    1. There is not one truth for theology and another for natural or philosophical knowledge.

    2. Therefore, we cannot sweep seeming contradictions under the rug; they must be resolved intellectually by the use of reason.

  B. Second is the doctrine of the Two Books—the Book of Scripture and the Book of Nature.

    1. These are two complementary ways in which God reveals himself to man.

    2. Because both books have the same ultimate author, they cannot contradict one another.

  C. Third is the recognition that both books require careful interpretation.

    1. St. Augustine wrote extensively about both the acquisition through the senses of natural knowledge and biblical interpretation.

    2. Biblical passages have layered meanings: for example, a literal, an allegorical, an anagogical, and a moral meaning.

    3. Literal interpretation did *not* mean what it does today; for example, St. Augustine's *Literal Interpretation of Genesis* denies a six-day, and even a six-period, creation.

    4. The Bible's ultimate divine authorship is partly obscured behind the human words expressed by human writers.

    5. Key to St. Augustine's thought, then, is the doctrine of accommodation: Biblical expressions were accommodated to the understanding of their original audience.

    6. Correct interpretation of either Scripture or the world requires the assiduous exercise of reason.

    7. Because biblical interpretation is very difficult, our explanations of some passages should be held only provisionally.

8. Because it is often easier conclusively to prove natural and philosophical propositions than interpretations of specific biblical passages, our interpretations of biblical passages must be informed by the current state of sure scientific and other knowledge.

9. Augustine's writings are full of scientific information gleaned from reading Classical sources or his own observations.

10. Failure to conform interpretations to the certain knowledge gained from other sources (such as the Book of Nature) opens the interpreter, and Christianity as a whole, to ridicule for being unlearned.

D. Fourth and finally, St. Augustine asserted that in terms of the pursuit of religion versus the pursuit of science or philosophy, religion has primacy, but scientific knowledge is a key *ancilla* ("handmaiden") that assists true religion.

1. This subordinate status is a reflection of the relative values given by society at the time to the two realms of inquiry.

2. Augustine stated that knowledge of the natural world both reveals the majesty of God's creation and is indispensable for correct biblical exegesis.

IV. The complex relationship between knowledge gained by faith and knowledge gained by reason is summarized in two opposing phrases: *Credo ut intellegam* ("I believe so that I may understand") and *Intellego ut credam* ("I understand so that I may believe.").

A. The terms come from a well-known sermon by St. Augustine; this issue appeared frequently in his writings.

B. Augustine concludes that the two are inseparable—they build on each other constantly. Neither can be slighted.

C. Working together, they can be mutually correcting, helping us attain *recta ratio* and *recta fides*—right reason and right faith.

V. In 1998, Pope John Paul II issued an important encyclical entitled *Fides et ratio* (*Faith and Reason*), which deals precisely with the issues at hand.

A. The document sketches a useful history of the relationship of faith and reason in theology; its teachings reaffirm St. Augustine's formulations.

1. It emphasizes the indispensability of both faith and reason, which it calls the "two wings on which the human spirit rises to the contemplation of truth."
2. Faith held simply and without the exercise of reason is condemned and "runs the grave risk of withering into myth or superstition."
3. *Fideism* (blind faith over reason) and *biblicism* (reliance on biblical texts alone) are explicitly rejected.

B. Likewise, unaided human reason is unable to attain or to prove the ultimate truths of existence; these are revealed through faith in the Christian revelation.
1. The faith statements that run most strongly throughout the document are not specific dogmas of Christianity but, rather, that "human life has meaning" and that "there exists an eternal and transcendent truth."
2. These two faith statements are taken as propositions to guide the exercise of reason.
3. Consequently, certain recent philosophical currents are criticized, including radical relativism, nihilism, and scientism.
4. Specifically in terms of science, warning is given that scientific studies uninspired by a faith in greater meanings risk devolving solely into means of material production or of other abuses.
5. The encyclical expresses an inherently optimistic view of humanity and human abilities, in opposition to recent pessimistic philosophical and cultural trends.

C. In sum, like Augustine, the document sees the two ways of gaining knowledge as inextricably linked; both are necessary for the pursuit of, and the belief in, the existence of truth.

Essential Reading:

Lindberg and Numbers, *God and Nature*, chapter 1 (pp. 19–48).

John Paul II, *Fides et ratio*.

Supplementary Reading:

St. Augustine, *Confessions*.

Questions to Consider:

1. Two philosophical currents, scientism (all true knowledge is attainable through science) and skepticism (the foundations of our knowledge are slim or inadequate), both undercut the faith-based knowledge claims found in religious thought. What happens, however, when skepticism is applied to scientism? Does science hold up better against skepticism than theology?

2. Choose any premise you hold as true (a knowledge claim) and consider why you hold it as true (for example, on what grounds) and how firmly you do so. Consider the foundations of your premise and supporting premises. Is there a point at which a "leap of faith" is required to undergird your premise? Consider how "far back" in your personal knowledge system this leap is positioned. Do you remain confident (that is, trusting) of it? Why or why not? Repeat with other premises.

Lecture Three—Transcript
Faith and Reason—Scripture and Nature

In our introductory lecture, we mentioned two methods of gaining knowledge claims: faith and reason. Now it's time to look at these two methods a little bit more closely. Faith operates by belief. A premise is stated and believed or accepted to be true, usually with the backing of some authority. The second—reason—operates by logical argument from premises to conclusions. In this lecture, we are going to examine these methods and their historical interrelationship. This lecture is foundational; it is going to provide for us a basis for our future lectures.

But besides faith and reason, these two methods, there is something else of equal importance that I haven't mentioned yet: namely, where did the premises that are subjected to them come from? So we need to look at sources as well—two sources of knowledge. The two I have in mind are nature—the natural world—and the scriptures. Nowadays we would consider these very different kinds of sources, but this was not always the case. We have to assess exactly how the two were used and related to one another. Let's take a look now in this lecture at the two sources, nature and the scriptures, and the two methods, faith and reason.

Much of the basic Christian understanding of these topics was worked out in the Patristic period. That is the age of the church fathers, the first, say, five centuries of the Christian era. The most important figure for Western Christianity is certainly St. Augustine of Hippo. He was born in North Africa in 354 to a Christian mother and a pagan father. What St. Augustine did that makes him so memorable is that he produced a profound and enduring synthesis between Greek philosophical knowledge—that is, reason—and Christian belief—that is, faith. And in so doing, he created systems and methods that are foundational to Christianity. I can't possibly overemphasize the importance of St. Augustine. His ways of thinking have become fully engrained into basic ways of thinking fundamental to Western culture. Augustine wrote an enormous amount; over five million of his words survive, and this includes over 100 books, 200 letters, and about 500 of the estimated 8,000 sermons he delivered in his life as a North African bishop.

As with all of us, St. Augustine's thought was conditioned by the times in which he lived and by his personal history, so it makes sense that we should start with a little bit of biography. As a young man, Augustine rejected Christianity because its teachings seemed absurd and illogical and the Bible full of fictions and absurdities. The version of Christianity he received was presumably predominantly from his mother, Monica. Her approach to religion was not an intellectual one; it was predominately faith-based, but this was clearly inadequate for the young Augustine, who, thinking all Christianity had to be this way, simply rejected it.

In turn, he turned to the Manichees. Now who on earth were the Manichees? The Manichees were a widespread sect. They were particularly popular in North Africa that rejected reliance on faith in favor of what could be proven by argument. So right there was something to attract the young intellectual Augustine. But more characteristic of the Manichees is their dualism; that is, they envisioned the world as a battleground between two forces: good and evil, light and darkness. The two are mixed in the world and in constant battle.

We are going to return to Manichaeism in future lectures because it's one of those ideas that keeps cropping up again and again, for whatever reason, down to the present day. But my point is that, right from the beginning, Augustine's life was marked by an interest in the relationship between faith and reason: at first, the faith presented to him by Monica and rejected, and the reason presented by the Manichees.

Augustine was a teacher of rhetoric and an avid reader. Time and time again throughout his autobiography, the *Confessions*, he refers to the enormous impact made on him by Classical texts: works by Cicero, by Aristotle, by the Stoics, by Plato, and particularly by the Neo-Platonists. He knew the Classical pagan tradition very well, and he benefited from it. Eventually, he left North Africa and traveled to Rome, where he had heard that students were better behaved, and in 384, accepted a job as professor of rhetoric in Milan. Actually, the students he found there were no better behaved than the ones he left in Africa, but poor guy.

While he was there, he went to hear the local bishop, Ambrose, preaching. Augustine wanted to hear Ambrose's celebrated rhetorical style, but Augustine found something different happening. He found himself listening to the words and their meaning, rather than just the way they were strung together. What he found to his amazement was that Ambrose could interpret passage after passage out of the scriptures in a way that they made sense. Augustine was astonished. And here began his lifelong interest in how to interpret the Bible correctly.

To finish Augustine's story, he was eventually baptized at Easter in the year 387; he returned to North Africa where he became a priest and then a bishop and continued to be a prolific writer until his death there in 430. With that contextualization in place, let's turn to four points made by St. Augustine in his voluminous writings. These not only became fundamental to Christian theology, but they're foundational, as I have said, to our study.

The first point is a very simple one: simply, that there is a unity of truth. There is not one truth for philosophy, one truth for science, one truth for theology. As Augustine says, and I quote him here, "There is no teacher of truth but God, no matter where it comes to light." Thus, with one teacher and one who, unlike his human counterparts, is both omniscient and always consistent, there must be a single truth.

What's the consequence? If the method of faith tells us one thing and the method of reason tells us another, then that disagreement has to be resolved. If nature tells us one thing and scripture tells us another, then that has to be resolved. We can't sweep these conflicts under the rug. We can't say, "Oh, well, that's fine for natural science, but faith tells me something different." It doesn't allow what I think is one of the more insipid lines that's sometimes heard coming out of the modern mouth, "Well you believe what you want. I'll believe what I want. Everyone's entitled to his opinion." This is a lazy and anti-intellectual copout. St. Augustine will have none of it: one God, one truth. The challenge, and Augustine stresses just how difficult this is, is for fallible human beings to get the truth right.

St. Augustine's other points flow from this fundamental unity of truth. Next comes his doctrine of the Two Books, the Book of Nature and the Book of Scripture. In one of his sermons, St. Augustine said, "Let the Bible be a book for you so that you may hear it. Let the sphere of the world be also a book for you so that you may see it." The idea is that God reveals himself to mankind in two qualitatively different ways by inspiring the sacred writers and by creating the world. We human beings can look at both to learn about God. Now since both books have the same ultimate author, there can't be any contradictions between them. In other words, truth from the Book of

Nature, what we call science now, cannot contradict with the truth from the Book of Scripture, that is, theology.

You might be saying to yourself by this point, "This is well and good, but isn't it blindly idealistic?" That is to say, surely there have been and surely there are conflicts between natural and theological knowledge or between knowledge gained by faith and knowledge gained by reason. Of course. And St. Augustine was well aware of this.

And that brings us in fact to Augustine's third point. Both of the books require careful interpretation. Apparent contradictions arise from incorrect interpretations. And Augustine in fact investigated the interpretation of both nature and the Bible. In terms of the Book of Nature, Augustine pondered at length the reliability of our senses to give us good information. He realized that even though the senses transfer to our minds exactly what it is they are sensing, our minds can be mistaken in the way they interpret the information that comes through the senses. Simply, things are not always what they seem. The real truth of the way things are is not necessarily provided by a simple application of the senses, so reading the Book of Nature can be difficult. It requires rational analysis; no scientist would disagree with that.

Augustine further argued, however, that properly understanding the scripture is even more difficult, and there are several reasons. First, biblical passages can have several meanings simultaneously: a literal, an allegorical, a moral meaning all at once. For Augustine—and this may surprise you—what's the most difficult? The literal meaning. That's the hardest one to get. Nowadays, we are quite familiar with claims of biblical literalists, most notably, for example, over the reading of the creation stories in the first two chapters of Genesis. For Augustine, and indeed for all theologians until relatively recent times, literal did not mean, as it means today, a surface meaning, what might be called "naïve" literalism. Instead, what it meant is an interpretation of a passage in such a way that it maintains its connection to the topic it seems to be describing and assigns meanings to the individual words so that the passage makes sense in relation to other sources of knowledge.

We need an illustration for that. Take Genesis I. The literal topic is clearly the creation of the world. Obviously the passage can be given analogical and other meanings to speak about morality or God's providence and so forth, but the literal sense must expound something, something that has to do with the creation of the world. It doesn't say how close it has to be to a surface text; it just has to retain the connection between the text and the obvious subject.

Augustine himself labored for years on a literal interpretation of Genesis I. Why did he have so much trouble? Because interpretation is hard. He was not going to be satisfied until his interpretation did two things: resolved contradictions in the text (for example, between the two discrepant accounts of the order of creation in Genesis I versus Genesis II) and two, provided an account of creation harmonious with both reason and knowledge from other sources. Thus, for example, Augustine's literal interpretation of Genesis denies entirely a six-day period of creation. Augustine's literalism is far from the naïve literalism that we encounter today.

Biblical interpretation requires just enough faith to believe that there is some truth hidden in the scriptures and, from that point on, requires the assiduous exercise of reason to get at that truth correctly. Principles that Augustine annunciated for biblical exegesis became general principles for Christian theology, and we will see them again and again in this course. He begins with the assumption, a faith statement, that the Bible has an ultimate divine authorship. But this ultimate authorship is partly obscured, he says, behind the human words expressed by the human beings who actually did the writing. In other words, the Bible is inspired, not dictated.

Secondly, biblical expressions are accommodated to their audience. This is known as the doctrine of accommodation. We should not expect scripture to confuse the audience—the original audience—with intricacies of mathematics or astronomy that are far beyond them. That's not its purpose. St. Thomas Aquinas, writing about 800 years after Augustine, would write that, "Scripture speaks according to the opinion of the people." However, we should be able to give some interpretation to any biblical passage to save its meaning by proper exegesis.

Third, because biblical interpretation is so difficult, our explanations of some particularly troublesome passages can be held only provisionally. Fourth and finally, Augustine notes that it is often easier to prove natural and philosophical propositions than it is to interpret specific biblical passages. We can, after all, do experiments to test natural hypotheses, and we have evidence that St. Augustine himself carried out some simple experiments. He mentions, in *The City of God*, playing around with magnets. He also mentions trying to test the Classical belief that the flesh of the peacock does not putrefy. He had a good command of the scientific knowledge of his day concerning astronomy, mathematics, botany, and so forth.

So, Augustine says, "Interpretation of biblical passages must be informed by the current state of demonstrable knowledge." This may surprise you, but Augustine was really prophetic when he warned explicitly about the danger of being ignorant or dismissive of demonstrated scientific knowledge. He writes very famously, "It is a disgraceful and a dangerous thing for an unbeliever to hear a Christian presumably giving the meaning of scripture and talking nonsense on these topics. Many non-Christians," he notes, "are well versed in natural knowledge, so they can detect," what he calls, "vast ignorance in such a Christian and laugh it to scorn." The danger is obvious. The failure to conform interpretations to demonstrated knowledge opens the interpreter and, by extension, Christianity as a whole, to ridicule for being unlearned.

There's a personal dimension here. Remember that Augustine was attached to the Manichees for almost a decade. How did he reject them in the end? It wasn't Ambrose's teaching or reading the Bible that did it. Instead, Augustine rejected the Manichees based on what he had learned of natural philosophy and mathematics. He tells us in the *Confessions* that Manichean doctrines included several regarding the nature of the world, particularly astronomy. But Augustine was familiar with the writings of the best Greek astronomers and mathematicians, and so that their writings were much more likely true, better demonstrated, better supported, than what the Manichees were saying to him. Yet he writes, "I was expected to believe what the Manichees had written, although it was entirely at variance with the principles of mathematics and the evidence of my own eyes." When Manichean teachers couldn't resolve his questions, the intellectually demanding Augustine left the sect. So Augustine was aware that knowledge of the natural world saved him from the Manichees and led him on his road to the true faith.

Now, you might ask, "why didn't Augustine just become a mathematician or a naturalist instead of a theologian?" This brings us to my fourth general point. He simply considered theological knowledge more important. Secular knowledge, such as natural philosophy, was considered an *ancilla*, that is, a hand-maiden that could assist true religion. *Ancilla* is the Latin word where we get "ancillary" in English from. So it wasn't something you would focus on for its own sake, but it could help in true religion. For Augustine, it is better for people with a limited time and intellectual energy—the average guy on the street—to get the eternal truths of religion first rather than crowding those out from a preoccupation for knowledge of the finite natural world.

In the case of scientific knowledge, Augustine states that it's indispensable, however, for those who want to carry out correct biblical exegesis. His writings show a realization that knowledge of the natural world by revealing the majesty of God assists faith and religious devotion. What about faith versus reason? What we've seen thus far is that Augustine puts a premium on the exercise of reason. Indeed, to those who would prevent people from using reason in religion, he exclaims, "Far be it from God to hate in us that faculty by which he made us superior to all other living things. And may it ever be far from us to believe in such a way that we do not accept or seek out reason. For we would not even be able to believe unless we had a soul that was endowed with reason."

What of faith? Augustine certainly doesn't leave that out. In a well-known sermon of his, he recounts a discussion. He tells a little anecdote, a discussion he held with a man who said to him, "Let me understand so that I may believe." Augustine's initial response was, "No. Believe so that you may understand." Well the two opposing Latin phrases used here, *Credo ut intelligam* and *Intellego ut credam* came to represent the dilemma of where do we start in our search for knowledge? Do we start with a faith statement? Do we start with reason? How do we actually get the ball rolling?

Augustine realized that his own journey towards faith required reason. And he recognized explicitly in this sermon that those 8,000 sermons of his could operate only on the understanding, that is, on reason, even though their ultimate goal was to create faith. Thus, he concluded that faith increases by understanding. The exercise of reason is necessary to what he calls, *recta fides*, right faith. But he also recognizes that the Manichees went wrong by denigrating faith. As Augustine wrote, "The church demands some things that should be believed, even though they cannot be proven." And this to him seemed better than, "The Manichees who laughed at people who took things on faith, promised proofs, and then proposed preposterous inventions in the guise of proofs." Thus Augustine recognized that faith and reason could not be separated, nor could one really be given the priority over the other. They always worked together.

He finishes his anecdote by saying, "Indeed, we agreed. Understand so that you believe and believe so that you understand." Reason could not reveal to us, for example, the mystery of the Trinity. But once faith ascends to the doctrine, then reason can refine and make plausible the belief. Similarly, faith cannot be gained in more than a tentative and really unsatisfactory way without a foundation that's based in reason. Moreover, both faith and reason are prone to error, but working together, they can prove mutually correcting, helping to attain for us what Augustine calls *recta fides*, right faith, and *recta ratio*, right reason. In Augustine's formulation, faith and reason cooperate incessantly to help us gain right knowledge from both the Book of Nature and the Book of Scripture.

Augustine's view is at odds with some modern ideas that faith and reason are opposed somehow or that the two are segregated into either theological or scientific pursuits: theology with faith, science with reason. So is Augustine's only a historical perspective that is now lost to the modern world? No, not at all. Let's now do what I am going to try and do in as many of these lectures as I can, that is, bring our historical discussions up to the present.

Let's bring St. Augustine's fifth century formulations up to the present day. In 1998, an importance encyclical—that is, a teaching document–was issued by Pope John Paul II. The document is entitled *Fides et Ratio*. That is, faith and reason. So it is clearly germane to our discussions. Indeed, I should point out that the engagement of faith knowledge with the modern world, particularly the scientific world, was a central interest of the late pope. I have to say this fact may come as a surprise to those who hear of papal statements only through the American news media that tends to cater to the lowest common denominator. In other words, theology and philosophy are too hard and only sex is of interest. But let that be.

The document presents views of faith and reason and their interactions that are very similar to St. Augustine's ideas. Indeed, it sketches a very useful history of the relationship between the two in theology. Like Augustine, it emphasizes the indispensability of both and their mutual support. In fact, it calls faith and reason, "the two wings on which the human spirit rises to the contemplation of truth." Given this commitment to both faith and reason, the letter takes aim equally at current trends that neglect either one or the other. First, it defends reason, particularly in a theological context. It condemns a position called fideism. Now fideism is a blind adherence to faith statements that ignores or even explicitly rejects the application of reason to them. In fideism, faith statements are not subjected to logical development or analysis or even to the simplest logical test of all, that of consistency and non-contradiction.

You may have seen a rather unfortunate bumper sticker that was popular a few years back that read, "God said it. I believe it. That settles it." Well that's one rather lowbrow expression of fideism. But the encyclical explains rather pointedly that faith statements held without any accompanying reason are flawed and precarious. "It is an illusion," the document reads, "that faith tied to weak reasoning might be more penetrating. On the contrary, faith then runs the grave risk of withering into myth or superstition." Strong words.

On the other side, in defending faith, the document expresses the conviction that faith acts as a necessary challenge to reason, spurring it on to ever greater heights and greater accomplishments by proposing to it transcendent truths that unaided reason could not reach and might not suspect actually exist. You might think that, at this point, a document written by the highest teaching authority of the largest Christian denomination would inject recognizably Christian creed statements. Interestingly enough, it does no such thing, for the faith statements that run most strongly through the document are not specific Christian doctrines, but rather such things as, "Human life has meaning" and "There exists an eternal and transcendent truth."

These faith statements are seen in the context of the document as central consequences of the Christian message and are taken as propositions needed to guide and to inspire the exercise of reason. So a consequence of this is a criticism of some modern philosophical trends. Here the document becomes very interesting, particularly to historians, because it attempts to chronicle the loss of implicit positive faith statements in academic philosophical discourse and modern culture. One example: radical relativism. The document says that this exists only because of a loss of faith in an ultimate truth towards which we are able to strive—even if we can't attain it— towards which we can strive.

This leads to the flawed belief that, "Truth is born only of consensus and not of a consonance between the intellect and objective reality." Similarly, nihilism—that nothing matters—results from a lack of faith in the purpose, meaning, and thus, the value of human existence. Pragmatism, too, is criticized because it's seen only as a fallback position, resulting from a loss of faith and the existence of transcendent ideals that are worth striving for.

Most germane to our subject, the validity of scientism is seriously questioned. Now scientism is a philosophical position that rejects as nonexistent all knowledge claims except those gained from the positive sciences; in short, that the sciences themselves can provide absolutely everything there is to know. There is nothing outside; in other words, there's nothing outside the ambit of the sciences.

By rejecting the possibility of greater meanings, of aesthetics, and ethics, scientism then has the danger of making the pursuit of science devolve solely into a means of material and economic production, rather than human enlightenment. And, as the document further says, can conflate the technologically possible with the morally permissible. Indeed, the document ends with an address specifically to scientists, to continue their work, their important work, while maintaining an openness to what is called the sapiential dimension of science: that is, its ability to contribute to wisdom, from the Latin *sapientia*, rather than just knowledge; that is, in addition to scientific facts and their applications, to remain aware of ideals, ethics, aesthetics, and meaning.

What's interesting to note is that the criticized movements don't actually result from a loss of faith per se, but rather a loss of positive faith. That is, human beings are totally unable—totally unable—to determine by reason whether or not there is a transcendent truth or an objective reality. Strong relativists, nihilists, and the rest make the faith-based claim that there is not. Weaker forms of these groups assert that because it's unknowable by reason, it's irrelevant. Thus to the latter, the encyclical proposes the advantages of faith. Why not just take on faith the existence of a transcendent truth and that gives you something towards which to strive. To the former group, the strong position of nihilism or relativism, it suggests replacing negative faith with positive faith.

Crucial to the papal position is the view that all these trends diminish human ability, human vision, human hope, and human striving, and thus, ultimately human culture and human life. The thing that I find really most remarkable about this document is its enormous optimism about humanity—may I say its enormous faith in humanity—in an age where we're much more accustomed to pessimism. It is necessary not to abandon the passion for ultimate truth, it declares, the eagerness to search for it or the audacity to forge new paths in the search. It is faith that stirs reason to move beyond all isolation and willingly run risks so that it may attain whatever is beautiful, good, and true. Faith cannot be seen as opposing reason, but rather, as the encyclical argues, faith thus becomes the convinced and the convincing advocate of reason. Faith inspires reason to go further than it might on its own and supports its powers.

In this lecture, we've seen that the interrelationship of faith and reason is complicated indeed. Augustine tackled several thorny issues and concluded that faith and reason are cooperative, not complimentary in the sense that one has one realm and another has a different one, but rather that both cooperate all the time in gaining knowledge of all sorts. His views were reaffirmed in a recent encyclical that provides an inspiringly optimistic view of human abilities and potential for obtaining knowledge.

In our next lecture, we will turn to another fundamental issue in the science-religion relationship, namely, to what extent is God active in the natural world?

Lecture Four
God and Nature—Miracles and Demons

Scope:

This lecture treats issues fundamental to the entire course, namely, the nature of causation and our ability to identify it accurately. A crucial point of contact between science and religion is the question of the extent of God's involvement in the running of the natural world. Theologians across time and denominations disagree widely on this point. Medieval theologians and natural philosophers, however, favored naturalistic explanations whenever possible, rather than recourse to divine intervention. The subject of miracles focused the issue, and the need to discern true miracles from superficially similar human, natural, or demonic marvels required scientific investigation of natural causes and, thus, instances a co-development of science and theology. Very importantly, one's views of the state of the spiritual world influence and form one's views toward the natural world and science.

Outline

I. The extent to which God is involved in the running of creation influences the role and importance assigned to natural science.

   A. The fundamental question is that of causation; is it natural, supernatural, or both?

   B. The Christian conception of a single, eternal, omnipotent God provides a necessary (though not sufficient) basis for science because it implies a regularity of action (that is, law-like behavior).

   C. Theological conceptions of how active God is in the running of creation span a broad range.

   1. At one end lies supernaturalism, which holds that God is the immediate cause of all effects.

   2. Some supernaturalism can be called "naïve"; that is, God is resorted to as a general explanation of the unknown. God's activities need not be regular.

   3. Such supernaturalism undermines trust in scientific laws and the use of reason to comprehend the world because nature functions at God's direct whim.

4. A more intellectually sophisticated form of supernaturalism is known as *occasionalism.* Occasionalism holds that all causation is directly from God's will and that the link we see between cause and effect is an artifact of our perceptions.

5. Occasionalism need not undermine science, because God is rarely conceived of as capricious. His constancy—a kind of a covenant with his creation—fills in for "laws of nature." Occasionalists see these laws as artifacts of God's uniform behavior.

6. God thus maintains, by the continuous exercise of his uniform activity, a *cursus communis naturae* ("common course of nature").

7. At the other end of the spectrum is *naturalism,* which holds that God's direct activity ceased after the creation—effects (and the *cursus communis naturae*) are caused by powers, laws, or "natures" that God initially implanted in things.

8. The two views are based on notions of primary and secondary causation. God is the primary cause; created things are secondary causes.

9. In fact, we cannot ascertain empirically the true nature of causation (that is, decide between naturalism and supernaturalism).

10. Both have been subject to criticism on logical grounds, and between these extremes exists a continuum of intermediate positions.

D. In general, traditional Christianity (particularly in the Middle Ages) holds a position on the naturalism side but not radically so.

1. Thirteenth-century theologians argued that although God can do anything he wishes, he chooses to restrict himself (almost always) within the *communis cursus naturae,* thus guaranteeing the validity of logical investigation in an (almost always) constant world.

2. This state of affairs runs contrary to much popular opinion, which erroneously believes that medievals had frequent recourse to supernatural activity for explanations.

3. Given the bent toward naturalism, orthodox Christian theology holds that God *almost* invariably works through "secondary causes."

4. Expositions of the creation of the world in the Middle Ages were often highly naturalistic; God's direct activity was, for some theologians, limited to an initial moment of *creatio ex nihilo*.

5. Some medievals (for example, the School of Chartres) also proposed naturalism to explain some biblical miracles, such as the parting of the Red Sea.

6. This choice of view guarantees an important place for scientific investigation of causes.

II. Miracles provide a crucial test case for views on God's activity in nature.

A. Although medieval thinkers favored naturalism, room had to be left for at least some miracles (for example, the Resurrection) affirmed by faith.

B. For most Christian theologian/natural philosophers, miracles somehow fall outside the *cursus communis naturae*.

C. The key problem lies in the discernment of miracles (how do we recognize a true miracle?) because: (a) a given phenomenon may have diverse causes, and (b) we may not recognize an apparently natural event as actually miraculous.

1. We can recognize a miracle only if we know natural causes extremely well; thus, a desire to verify miracles leads to scientific inquiry.

2. Miracles can show a naturally inexplicable disproportion between cause and effect; thus, the power of natural causes must be known.

3. Advances in scientific understanding, by teaching us the limit of natural actions, bear upon the discernment of miracles.

4. This is one example of the co-development of science and religion.

III. Protestants (especially Anglicans) invented the doctrine of the cessation of miracles—that the "age of miracles" ceased with the apostolic generation.

A. This doctrine was promulgated largely to discredit Catholicism, which held that miracles not only continued to occur but continued to testify to truth of the Catholic faith.

B. Shorn of the evidential power of miracles, some Protestant thinkers of the 17th century—including well-known natural philosophers—turned to the investigation of witch and demon activity in order to gather evidence of the spirit realm (see Lecture Seven).

C. Demonic activity was already of great interest to theologians and natural philosophers.

   1. Demons cannot perform miracles but only trick us into thinking that they can.

   2. In orthodox Christian theology, demons do *not* have supernatural power (contrary to modern popular opinion).

   3. They do, however, know natural laws perfectly, and being incorporeal, they can move with infinite speed. Thus, they *appear* to work miracles, but their actions are natural.

   4. A very learned human being could do nearly as well as demons; hence, the power of technology to produce *marvels* but not *miracles*.

IV. Some recent forms of Christianity exemplify the link among views of God's activity in the world, miracles, and trust in scientific inquiry.

  A. Some non-mainstream American fundamentalist sects greatly enhance the frequency and importance of "miracles" (a kind of crude occasionalism) and, consequently, diminish natural causation and the scope of scientific frameworks.

  B. Further, they attribute far greater power to Satan and demonic forces than is orthodox and, thus, border on (or even fall into) Manichean dualism.

   1. Consequently, their spiritual world is disordered, reflected in an irregular natural world (full of interventions) and a lack of faith in the regularities that constitute science.

   2. It is not surprising that these same sects are those that most consistently oppose scientific inquiry, explanation, and education.

Essential Reading:

Lindberg and Numbers, *God and Nature*, chapter 2 (pp. 49–75).

Supplementary Reading:

Amos Funkenstein, *Theology and the Scientific Imagination*.

Questions to Consider:

1. How would the status of miracles differ in a supernaturalist versus a theistic naturalist view of the world? Think about how the *cursus communis naturae* is generated in each.

2. Imagine that God suspended all his activity for an indeterminate (but finite) period of time; how would this appear to us? Assume first that naturalism is the correct description of the world; then assume an occasionalist (supernaturalist) perspective. Could the suspension of God's activity for a time help us decide between naturalism and supernaturalism? (Hint: Think about how we sense.)

Lecture Four—Transcript
God and Nature—Miracles and Demons

If we assume that a creator God exists, then we have to ask, how involved is he in the running of his creation? This is a crucial question for the relationship between science and theology. It asks to what extent the world operates on its own according to inherent laws and natures and to what extent God involves himself in the process. It's a basic question about causation: what causes the phenomena that we see? Really, this is the essential question, the central question of scientific inquiry: the discovery of causes.

But it's also a question for theologians. Why? How God is involved in the running of creation influences the way we study the natural world. It's been suggested, for example, that the concept of a single eternal omnipotent God provides a necessary, although not a sufficient, basis for science as we know it. This is because God— such a god—can be taken to imply regularity, which is what scientific study endeavors to uncover. In contrast, think about a pantheon of quarreling lesser gods, always doing and undoing each other's work. That would tend to undermine confidence in the regularity and predictability of natural processes.

Within Christianity, there is a range of historical answers to the question of God's activity. At one end of the spectrum lies the position called supernaturalism. This says that God directly affects everything in the world. Simply put, all causation is supernatural. It comes from a power outside of nature rather than powers within nature. All events and phenomena are caused immediately by God.

Within this one position, there are several sub-positions. One is what I will call "naïve" supernaturalism, where the answer to all questions of causation is simply one word: God. Often this sort of naïve supernaturalism comes from ignorance or a lack of interest in, or even a contempt for, natural investigations and explanations. But there's also a much more sophisticated version of supernaturalism, which is called occasionalism. According to this system, the links that we witness between cause and effect—for example, the water in a tea kettle put over the fire grows hot because it's over the fire—are merely consequences of our perceptions. The fire has no inherent ability to heat water. Instead, it's the result of God's direct intervention. Indeed, the term "occasionalism" arises from a fundamental tenet to this position, namely that one thing doesn't actually cause another; it only marks the occasion at which God acts.

Supernaturalism, in general, potentially diminishes one's interest in the natural world. If there is no causative power resident in nature, then why should we bother studying it? Supernaturalism can also undermine trust in scientific laws because the laws themselves have no real existence. But this is not the only perspective on supernaturalism. Thoughtful Christians, some of whom have been occasionalists, have almost never conceived of God as capricious. He acts in uniform and stable ways, according to a kind of a covenant that He established with the world when He created it. This covenant then fills in for the laws of nature. Another way of saying this is that God constantly creates, by his direct action, a *cursus communis naturae,* a common or usual course of nature.

On the other hand of the spectrum from supernaturalism lies the position that God's direct activity ceased after the creation. Now this can be supported by appeal to the verse in Genesis I, "On the seventh day he rested." That is to say we're still dwelling now in that extended seventh day when God is at rest. Under this conception, the effects and phenomena we witness are caused by inherent powers, laws, or natures that God implanted in things originally. This view is known as "naturalism," that is, causation is natural; it flows from natural things. God delegated, in a sense, some of his power to the things he created, endowing them with specific powers of causation. So fire heats the water in the kettle because God created fire in such a way that he gave to it the power of heating. In this case, the *cursus communis naturae* is the direct result of natural causes operating regularly and independently.

A way to describe the difference between God's direct and his mediated activity was annunciated by medieval theologians. They defined two levels of causation: primary and secondary. All Christians agree that God is the ultimate cause of all that is; all created things came ultimately from His creative act. And therefore they are secondary to Him. Thus, if they have inherent powers of causation, those powers are secondary. Supernaturalists now rely upon primary causation: the direct cause of effect is the first cause, that is, God. Naturalists, on the other hand, invoke secondary causation; the direct causes of effects are secondary causes, the regular activity of natural created things.

In a sense, what we're arguing about here is how many intermediaries we are going to have between God and the daily running of creation. A supernaturalist would say none. A naturalist would say some, although exactly how many depends upon your particular ideas about naturalism. For a supernaturalist, if God decides to go on a vacation or just to stop acting, things stop happening, or even existence stops happening. For a naturalist, the powers implanted in natural things would still continue to cause their usual effect.

A key point to notice here is that we, as human beings, cannot decide ultimately which is the true description of objective reality. There is no empirical test that's possible. All we can observe are effects and a temporal relationship between cause and effect. We can't actually demonstrate an operational connection between what we sense as a cause and what we witness as an effect.

Between the extremes of naturalism and supernaturalism exists a continuum of intermediate positions. Theologians and natural philosophers alike have positioned themselves at various points along this continuum, and it bears saying at this point that Christians are not alone in these discussions. A large group of Muslim theologians, most particularly the 11th-century al-Ghazzali, espoused a strongly occasionalist perspective. And that view was opposed from the other end of the spectrum in the 12th century by both his co-religionist, Ibn-Rushd, known as Averroës, and by the Jewish philosopher, Moses ben Maimon, known as Maimonides. In fact, the arguments of Ibn-Rushd and Maimonides were carefully studied by Christians in the Latin Middle Ages and deeply influenced their thinking on these issues. So if it needs to be said, I will just take the opportunity to point out that the works of the theologians of the three Western monotheistic religions were in fact mutually influential, and this is a point that's much too easily overlooked.

But let me get back to my point about the spectrum between naturalism and supernaturalism. There are objections to both extremes. Naïve supernaturalism of a sort that invokes God as immediate cause, but without any kind of commitment to uniformity of action, flies in the face of our daily experience—our experience of the orderly law-like behavior of nature. The occasionalist perspective that is a more sophisticated kind of supernaturalism preserves our experience of the uniformity of nature, but to some, it seemed to degrade God into a general factotum, constantly acting as the mechanic of the universe and bound to observe certain laws of action.

Worse, it seems to implicate, or it can be interpreted as implicating, God in evil acts. For example, if we used fire not to make tea, but for arson and murder, the immediate cause of the evil result would be God, not the reprobate who applied the fire to that end. At the other end, naturalism helps make sense of the world, explaining law-like behaviors, but in its extreme form, it can be seen as anti-providential determinism. What do I mean by that? By that, I mean that if the laws and powers in nature are set by God and remain absolutely unchanged and untouched, there seems to be no room left for God's providential care or intervention in the world. Indeed, in some cases, it risks treading on God's omnipotence, for having created and established the world in a particular way, he cannot step in to alter or suspend it. To some, this ran the risk of rendering God unnecessary after the initial creation.

How did these positions play out historically? In traditional Christianity, occasionalism was always a minority position. As for naïve supernaturalism, that was rejected already in the Patristic period. The clear counterargument to naïve supernaturalism is that, yes, God can do anything like turn a cucumber into an aardvark, but we don't see all possible things happening in the world. In fact, if you think about it, what we see happening in the world is a very, very small number of all the events that would be possible in a world where anything could happen.

Indeed, naïve supernaturalism's appeals to God's omnipotence were answered in a definitive way in the 13th century by theologians such as Alexander of Hales, St. Albert the Great, and his student, St. Thomas Aquinas. Now building on arguments from earlier theologians, they distinguished two different kinds of divine power. The first is merely God's omnipotence, and this is called the *potentia Dei absoluta*, the absolute power of God. The other is a subset of this. These are the powers that God actually chooses to exercise given the creation the way he made it. This is called the *potentia Dei ordinata*, God's ordained power. So while in the *potentia absoluta* God could turn a cucumber into an aardvark, because of the way he chose to create the world in the beginning, namely to make a world in which cucumbers don't turn into aardvarks, that power is not part of his *potentia ordinata*.

In brief, said St. Thomas, it's ridiculous to say that God does something just because he can. So while God could be capricious, while God could intervene constantly to change the laws of nature, and while he could turn cucumbers into aardvarks, he chooses not to. Thus mainstream Christian theology has historically held the position decidedly on the naturalism side, but not radically so.

Medieval thinkers preferred to appeal to nature for explanations of natural things, rather than resorting to the first cause, God. Created things do have powers of their own to cause effects, but, God can intervene directly in the world even though this is extremely rare. Recourse to God's direct action, for example, throwing up one's hands in the search for a causal explanation and saying, "Well, God did it, he can do anything," was not seen as a satisfactory answer. This state of affairs, I should point out, runs contrary to a lot of popular opinion that erroneously believes that the medievals had frequent recourse to supernatural explanation. This might have been the case among the medieval peasants, but not among intellectuals, the theologians.

An example of medieval Christian preference for naturalistic causation appears in commentaries on the creation. This might strike you as a strange place to look for naturalism, but actually it's not. It's a point of dogma that God created what is *ex nihilo*, that is, out of nothing. That of course had to be his direct act because prior to creation there was nothing but God and therefore no possible secondary causation. But many writers favored only an initial primary causation by God. St. Augustine, for example, argued for an instant of creation, one infinitesimal moment of direct divine causality, and in that instant, God brought something into existence out of nothing, which contained within itself what he called *semina* in Latin, or seeds, of things that were to be. These seeds were the created and specified powers that God implanted in creation in the initial creative act. And just as a seed contains within itself the power of producing a mature plant given time, so after God's initial instant of creation, the seeds began to produce, on their own, new forms according to their ordained powers.

Others, such as the natural philosopher theologians of the 11th and 12th century school of Chartres, dispensed with Augustine's *semina* while retaining a mere instant of creation. According, for example, to Thierry of Chartres, God created in that primordial instant only a confused primordial chaos composed of the four elements (fire, air, earth, and water in the medieval conception). But by their very act of creation, these elements were endowed with particular properties—for example, fire being hot and earth being heavy—and these native properties then took over the completion of the cosmos. Differences in density caused the elements to separate out, and this separation then caused a rotation of the cosmos, which we still see in the heavenly bodies today.

This motion in turn produced heat, and that heat, acting upon earth, which had agglomerated with water at the center of the universe from the settling out of the initially created elements, generated plants, animals, and finally man. Thierry's younger contemporary, William of Conches, goes a bit further, saying that since the same earth, water, and heat continue to exist today, then there's no natural reason why new human races are not produced naturally from their interaction. He concludes that since we've never seen this happen, then there must be some kind of divine prohibition against it.

Now here's a very curious inversion of 21st-century expectations. We have a 12th-century Christian writer at a cathedral school invoking God not to create living beings, but rather to prevent it from happening naturally. An important place for naturalism is in miracles. Some medievals tried to explain even biblical miracles naturalistically, but we have to be careful exactly how we say that because the topic is subtle and very important.

Take for example, the parting of the Red Sea, as described in Exodus. Scripture states that there was "a strong east wind that swept the sea throughout the night." Thus, this gave medieval commentators the opportunity to argue that it was the wind that divided the sea, not the direct finger of God. Get those images from Cecil B. Demille out of your head. They'll just confuse you. Thus, the general commitment to naturalistic explanations meant that God could be one step or more removed even from miracles. God might have parted the sea directly, that is, as an immediate cause, or instead, God, who had initially created air and wind with specific properties, such as the ability to push and dry up water, worked through secondary causes. And this is crucial to orthodox Christian theology, which states that God works almost invariably through secondary causes. Now this choice of theological perspective has an important consequence on the way we study the natural world. It elevates the status of created things by giving them both inherent powers and instrumentality in the hand of God. It makes them, in short, worth studying. Thus, it guarantees an important place for naturalistic investigations of created things and their properties and for the investigation of causes.

Let's take a little further illustration. Let's say you happen to be standing on the eastern shore of the Red Sea. Suddenly this tremendous wind whips up. Off flies your hat and the wind continues blowing throughout the night like you've never seen it before. After a while you look up at the sea and you see this finger of dry land extending far out into it. What happened? Surely you would point to the unusual wind as the immediate cause. You rightly enough think it to be an amazing event, but a fully natural one. Eventually, you look out and on the horizon you see a straggling group of people making their way towards you. When the man in front is within earshot, you yell out, "Wow! That's some wind, eh?" And he shouts back, "It's a miracle." Well you're puzzled because you witnessed the wind. You're satisfied that the effect was caused by it. So how can you settle the dispute? Was this a miracle or not? This is the sticky issue of the discernment of miracles: how to recognize miracles and how they fit into the course of nature. This is an important issue for theology and natural philosophy.

First, we need a definition of what actually constitutes a miracle. That was worked out by theologians over time. Moderns, attuned to science as paradigmatic of knowledge, forget or don't realize that theology, like science, is not static. It develops as theologians develop new ideas, arguments, and perspectives. Theology, like science, is about our desire to know, about our struggles to understand. Well, by the time of St. Thomas in the 13th century and owing in part to his thought, miracles were defined as special events outside the *cursus communis naturae*. These might be worked by God intervening directly, for example, in the initial creation or by his applying existing secondary causes in a special way, like wind to part the sea.

Discerning a true miracle is tricky for two reasons. First, a given phenomenon might have more than one possible cause, and it would be hard for us to determine what the cause is. Second, the result of a miracle might be a purely natural event, and so it's difficult to recognize that there's anything unusual about it. Well, let's return to the Red Sea. To determine whether or not the event we witnessed is a true miracle, we have to determine if it falls outside the *cursus communis naturae*, the common course of nature.

The consequence for the science-religion issue is profound. It means that we have to know as much as possible about the common course of nature; thus, the need to identify miracles leads directly into a need for scientific knowledge. Things are never easy, for our understanding of what constitutes the common course of nature is built up incrementally from our collective experiences. Therefore, when we come up against very rare phenomena for the first time, they can initially appear to be miraculous.

Then we need to turn to the central issue of this lecture, namely, causation. An event that displays a naturally inexplicable disproportion between the power of the evident cause and the effect is likely to be miraculous. Thus it requires us to know about and to quantify the power of natural agents. In this case, is the action, the power of wind, enough to produce a dry passage through the Red Sea? If the answer is no, then we might have a miracle via God's direct causation. If the answer is yes, then we still might have a miracle, but via God's manipulation of secondary causes, unless we can show that this kind of wind appears from time to time. Now here, the fact that a rare wind appeared just as a throng of nervous Israelites stood on the far shore increases the probability that it's miraculous. But since we cannot know causes with absolute certainty, our final answer can only be in probabilities.

And St. Thomas concludes that absolute identification of something as a miracle is, in the final analysis, ultimately an act of faith. The key point is that scientific understanding by teaching us the limits of natural actions is crucial to the discernment of miracles. Thus, here is one clear overlap between natural and theological inquiry and knowledge: the need to discern miracles encourages the study of natural laws and agencies. The knowledge of natural laws and agencies in return bears upon the discernment of miracles. The case of miracles is one example of the co-development of science and theology.

Miracles became a particular problem theologically and scientifically in the 17th century because at that time, after the Reformation, some Protestants, particularly Anglicans, adopted the doctrine of the cessation of miracles, namely that the age of miracles was over. It ended with the death of the apostolic generation. There's a practical motive here; the idea could discredit Catholicism, which held that miracles continue to occur and continue to testify to the particular truth of the Catholic faith.

However, as with many things, there were unintended consequences. Without the evidential, that is, the testimonial power of miracles, some Protestant thinkers of the 17th century turned to the investigation instead of witch and demon activity in order to gather evidence for the existence of a spirit realm. Several well-known natural philosophers participated in this endeavor. We'll talk more about that in our seventh lecture. But for now, it's worth talking a little bit more about demons and miracles. Demonic activity was of great interest to both theologians and natural philosophers because it provided a counterexample or a counterpoint to questions about God's activity in the world. The orthodox theological position states that demons do not have the power to produce true miracles. They can only trick us into thinking that they can. This is because demons don't have supernatural power. That is not something that God, who is the sole possessor of supernatural power, ever gave to them.

Demons do however know natural laws perfectly. They've been around a long time; they've been able to study them; they know them. And being incorporeal, they can move with infinite speed. Think about it. An incorporeal being has no dimensions, therefore it's not restricted to three-dimensional space as we know it, which is the domain of corporeal substances, so they can move—if that's even the right word—between points A and points B without ever being in between. Thus demons can appear to work miracles, but all they can really do is go and get natural agents. They know where they are, and they know how to get them and apply those agents to particular subjects in an instant.

So we are returned to the critical issue of discernment. What looks like a miracle might not be, and the dangerous part of it is assenting to the wrong miracle might put you within the power of demons. Significantly, since demonic action is entirely natural—that is, it relies on knowledge of natural causes and powers—a very learned human being could do nearly as well as a demon, except for the part, of course, of moving with infinite speed. Hence, knowledge of the natural world—what we call science—gives even human beings a power to produce seeming miracles. In short, we have a word for this: it's technology, which can produce marvels but not true miracles.

In my last minutes, let me apply what we've learned in a new direction. Some recent forms of Christianity exemplify the link I've been trying to talk about between views of God's activity in the world, miracles, and trust in scientific inquiry. I am referring to certain non-mainstream sects that greatly enhance the frequency and importance of miracles. They have miracles, for example, broadcast nightly on television, and their members are taught to expect a miracle in the way the rest of us expect the afternoon post. In some, they adopt the position of naïve supernaturalism, where God is constantly intervening in a way that is also erratic. Such a position, as we've seen, diminishes the role of natural causation and the scope of scientific explanation.

Further, in what we can now recognize really as a related development, many of the same groups attribute a far greater power to Satan and demonic forces than is acceptable in orthodox Christianity, to the point that their worldview borders on, if not falls into, Manichean dualism. Turn on the television in some places and you are likely to hear very frequent references to the power of Satan and the battle between good and evil forces, much as the Manichees would have expounded it to a skeptical St. Augustine.

As a result of this weak discernment criteria for miracles and a dualist mentality, their spiritual and corporeal worlds are disordered. The spiritual world is disordered by a supposed struggle between God and forces aligned against him. All you have to do is think, as St. Augustine did, what it would actually mean to oppose omnipotence. Think about that for a moment.

Indeed, the situation is little different from what I mentioned at the start of this lecture regarding a squabbling pantheon. The natural world is similarly disordered because it's so full of divine interventions that there's little sense in seeking out and trusting to a *cursus communis naturae*, a common course of nature; the regularities that, in fact, constitute science.

Given this situation, it's not surprising that these same sects are frequently the very ones that most consistently oppose or devalue scientific inquiry and the power of science to give explanations. As I said before, one's view of God's activity in the natural world orients one's view of natural science.

Now we have to move on. The past two lectures dealt with broad themes in theology and their impact on studies of the natural world. In the next two lectures, we are going to shift gears to examine a particular event in the science-religion interaction. Indeed, one of the best known episodes, the case of Galileo. You may discover that the best known things can also be the least understood.

Lecture Five
Church, Copernicus, and Galileo

Scope:

The "Galileo affair" is undoubtedly the most often-cited incident in the history of science-religion interactions. Far from being a simple case of science versus religion, however, it is extremely complex and brings up a host of important philosophical, scientific, and other issues that must be understood in context. In this lecture, we look at the background to these events in Copernicus's heliocentric theory, then detail the intricate events of 1613–1616—"Act I" of the Galileo affair—and their implications and possible explanations.

Outline

I. The "Galileo affair" is undoubtedly the most often-cited incident in the history of science-religion interactions.

    A. Although often presented as a simple "conflict" of religion against science, it is actually extremely complex, involving intellectual, philosophical, political, social, and personal clashes that far transcend in scope, interest, and importance any simplistic (and usually propagandistic) science-versus-religion readings.

    B. We will address three historical events in this and the following lecture:

        1. The background in terms of the proposal of Copernicus's heliocentric-geokinetic theory.

        2. The first phase of the Galileo affair (1613–1616) and its implications.

        3. The second phase of the Galileo affair (1632–1633), which ended in Galileo's conviction, recantation, and house arrest, and its implications.

II. In 1543, Nicholas Copernicus published his *De revolutionibus orbium coelestium*, which argued that, contrary to the prevailing Ptolemaic-Aristotelian system, the Sun was at the center of the universe (heliocentrism) and the Earth revolved around it (geokineticism).

    A. Copernicus delayed publication but was urged into publishing by several churchmen.

     1. He dedicated the work to Pope Paul III.

     2. Copernicus was himself in Holy Orders (a canon), and his astronomical expertise was sought out by Church officials to help reform the calendar.

B. Copernicus's theory found little acceptance.

     1. It violated commonsense experience and 2,000 years of astronomical theory and subverted fundamental principles of physics.

     2. No observational data supported it; predicted phenomena from a moving Earth (parallax) could not be observed.

     3. More literal readers of Scripture found it contradictory of clear passages, such as Joshua's miracle of making the *Sun* (not the Earth) stand still.

III. The first phase of the Galileo affair occurred in 1613–1616.

A. In 1613, Galileo's student Fr. Benedetto Castelli was asked by the Grand Duchess Christina (mother of Galileo's patron) about conflicts between Galileo's geokinetic theory and the Bible.

     1. The key biblical passage is the story of Joshua stopping the Sun to lengthen the day; other passages imply a stationary Earth and moving Sun.

     2. Castelli told Galileo about the event, and Galileo replied with a letter describing his position; Galileo eventually wrote a much longer letter to Christina.

     3. Galileo argued that Scripture had to be interpreted in the light of scientific knowledge; its expressions were accommodated to the original audience; and the literal meaning could be saved thanks to his own discovery of the Sun's rotation, which, he suggested, powered the planets.

B. On 20 December 1614, the Dominican friar Tommaso Caccini preached a sermon at Santa Maria Novella in Florence; he expounded the Joshua passage, then criticized Copernicus, mathematicians, and Galileo's followers.

C. The Inquisition was pulled in a few months later when another Florentine Dominican, Niccolò Lorini (who had attacked Galileo two years earlier), wrote a letter of complaint to the head of the Index and forwarded a copy of Galileo's letter to Castelli.

1. Galileo's letter was found to have some "bad expressions" but no serious objections. Two of the three "bad expressions" exist only in Lorini's copy, not in Galileo's original, suggesting that someone (Lorini?) was trying to make Galileo look bad.
2. Caccini was questioned; he claimed that Galileo's disciples held (seriously) heretical beliefs.
3. Persons named by Caccini were questioned, and Caccini's serious accusations were found groundless.
4. But the Inquisition convened a panel of consultants to examine the geokinetic thesis. On 24 February 1616, the panel advised that Copernicanism was "foolish and absurd" in philosophy and "heretical" in theology.
5. The Inquisition took no action on the recommendation.
6. However, the Index suspended circulation of Copernicus's book "until corrected." These "corrections" involved deleting passages offering interpretations of Scripture and claiming Copernicanism to be literally true.
7. Cardinal Roberto Bellarmino, one of the most powerful churchmen of the day in Rome and a highly important theologian, was told to give Galileo a verbal warning not to continue to hold Copernicanism as literally true. Galileo agreed.

D. Understanding this result requires some further background, especially regarding Bellarmino.
   1. In early 1615, a Neapolitan priest named Paolo Antonio Foscarini published a book reinterpreting the Bible to be compatible with Copernicanism.
   2. He sent a copy to Bellarmino; his reply is crucial background to the Galileo affair.
   3. Bellarmino praised Foscarini (and Galileo) for speaking "suppositionally and not absolutely," because declaring the absolute truth of the hypothesis would be "dangerous."
   4. However, he also claimed that *if* there were an undeniable demonstration of the Earth's motion, then Scripture would have to be reinterpreted carefully.
   5. Galileo, who had gone to Rome and who knew Bellarmino personally, apparently got a copy of Bellarmino's letter and wrote a rebuttal.

6. When the Index suspended Copernicus's book, it condemned Foscarini's.

IV. Examination of this first phase reveals a wealth of issues to be considered.

    A. Biblical interpretation seems to be a key issue, but even this is not straightforward.

        1. Galileo's writings show an exemplary understanding of accepted (Augustinian) principles of biblical exegesis.

        2. Earlier authors had reinterpreted the same passages without incident; thus, there is something special about Galileo and his time.

        3. To stave off further schism in the aftermath of the Reformation (which emphasized "personal interpretations" of Scripture), the Council of Trent (where Bellarmino was a key figure) forbade the reinterpretation of Scripture "contrary to the consensus" of the patristic writers.

        4. The fact that Foscarini published similar material at the same time may have aggravated the case.

        5. Galileo (and Foscarini) violated "intellectual turf" by claiming that his biblical interpretations were superior to those of theologians, especially while he told theologians to stay out of natural philosophy.

    B. Bellarmino conceded that a sound demonstration of the Earth's motion would lead to reinterpretation, but Galileo had no such proof.

        1. Galileo's telescopic "proofs"—the Jovian satellites and the phases of Venus—are inconclusive.

        2. Galileo's favored "proof"—that the tides are caused by the motion of the Earth—is completely wrong.

        3. Although Galileo was ultimately correct about heliocentrism, he was wrong to claim he had proof of it.

        4. Confusion would result if the Scriptures had to be reinterpreted for every *possible* (unproven) scientific system.

    C. Galileo might also have been caught in a power struggle between rival intellectual elites—Dominicans and Jesuits. Galileo's accusers were all Dominicans, and Galileo was on good terms with the Jesuits, who had verified his telescopic observations.

D. We are not free to indulge in collectivism by extending the actions of specific churchmen into a generalized statement about Galileo versus "the Church" (much less about science versus religion); there were clergy, theologians, and officials *on both sides* of the issue.

E. Finally, we have also to consider the larger issue of the nature of scientific knowledge (see Lecture Six).

V. After everything had been settled, final developments set the stage for developments 15 years later.

A. Galileo asked for an audience with the pope. The pope acknowledged that Galileo had certain enemies but stated that both he and the cardinals thought well of him and that Galileo could "feel safe as long" as the pope lived.

B. Galileo heard that rumors about his having been "condemned" were circulating and asked Bellarmino for a certificate setting out exactly what had been done.

Essential Reading:

Maurice A. Finocchiaro, *The Galileo Affair*, pp. 1–69, 87–118, 134–153.

Supplementary Reading:

Finocchiaro, *The Galileo Affair*, pp. 70–86.

Lindberg and Numbers, *God and Nature*, chapter 3 (pp. 76–113).

Questions to Consider:

1. Much of the first part of the Galileo affair deals with the issue of personal interpretations of Scripture. Consider the issue of personal interpretations. If theology is intended to give us objectively true knowledge, should personal interpretations of the Book of Scripture (resulting in theological knowledge) be handled or considered any differently from personal interpretations of the Book of Nature (resulting in scientific knowledge)?

2. In his "Letter to Christina," to what extent does Galileo mark out an intellectual sphere for natural philosophers in which he considers theologians are not permitted to tread? Given that the role and distinctness of the natural philosopher were not clear at this time, how would Galileo's thoughts be viewed? What would be the results of taking his advice?

Lecture Five—Transcript
Church, Copernicus, and Galileo

Whenever the topic of science and religion comes up, the issue of Galileo and the church is never far behind. This episode, that scholars have taken to calling the "Galileo affair," has been subject to use and abuse in historical writing, as well as on the stage, for many years.

In this and the following lecture, we are going to try to recapture and recontextualize some of the very interesting issues that are in play in the Galileo affair. We are going to focus on characters and the context and what the Galileo affair actually did in the course of science and religion. It is a complicated affair with lots of players and lots of twists of fortune. It's almost like a soap opera, in fact, an Italian soap opera. Scholars who have devoted their life to studying the issue still continued to debate some of the points that remain controversial.

The first thing I am going to do is divide our work for these two lectures into three parts. First, we need to get a handle on the scientific background to Galileo's affair. Second, we need to examine the first phase of the Galileo affair, which took place from 1613 to 1616. It's not always recognized that the Galileo affair actually had two separate periods of time that were separated by 15 years. In the next lecture, we are going to cover the second phase, and that took place in 1632 to1633. Let's start with the background.

For this we have to return to the mid-16th century. In 1543, Nicholas Copernicus published his *De revolutionibus orbium coelestium*, that is, *On the Revolution of the Heavenly Orbs*. In this book, Copernicus proposed two radical changes to man's conception of the cosmos. The first of the claims was heliocentrism, namely, that the sun is at the center of the solar system, or of the universe in Copernicus's mind. The second one was geokineticism, meaning simply that the earth is in motion. And the earth in fact has two motions: one, its diurnal motion on its axis and second, its annual motion around the sun. This was in contradistinction to the Ptolemaic-Aristotelian cosmos that was geocentric, earth at the center, and geostatic, earth not moving.

Copernicus had been working on these ideas for about 30 years. Already by 1514, he'd written a short summary of his ideas. He didn't publish this, but it circulated in manuscript and established his reputation as an astronomer to the extent that Pope Leo X in 1515 invited him to come to Rome to help work out the reform of the calendar that was then a pressing problem. Actually, Copernicus declined to do this because he said that our measurements for the length of the year were not accurate enough yet.

Copernicus might never have published his ideas if it hadn't been for the nagging of several fellow churchmen to do so. I say "fellow" churchmen since Copernicus himself was in Holy Orders. He was a canon of the cathedral in Krakow. A canon is a largely administrative office. Copernicus eventually published, but he passed the publication work off to others to finish for him. We will talk more about that in a bit.

Once Copernicus's theories were published, people didn't suddenly say, "Oh wow, why didn't we think about this before?" In fact, Copernicus's theory found little acceptance. Why? Several reasons. First, the moving earth and central sun violated commonsense experience. We don't feel the earth moving under our feet, and then we have no way to detect it. Second, Copernicus essentially threw out 2,000 years of coherent astronomical theory. A move like this in any field would not be welcomed. Third, it subverted fundamental principles of physics, such as the motion of heavy bodies towards the earth. Aristotle had put the earth at the center of the cosmos because it's the heaviest substance, and therefore anything that we drop that's heavy also falls towards the center.

So if you accept this crazy idea of Copernicus that the earth is somehow removed from the center and suspended away from the center, why then do heavy bodies still fall towards it? Why don't they go falling towards the sun, if the sun is at the center? So even if you accepted this, there were still some problems with Copernicus; namely, it predicted stellar parallax, but no one could see this. In fact, it took until the 19th century before it was actually detected.

On a totally different level, some readers of scripture found Copernicus's system contradictory to some clear passages in the Bible, such as the miracle in the Old Testament where Joshua makes the sun stand still in order to lengthen the day. The objections against heliocentrism and geokineticism were so compelling that for over 50 years after the publication of *De revolutionibus*; there were probably no more than 10 or maybe a dozen people who actually accepted Copernicanism. Many others, however, adopted Copernicanism as what we might call a "convenient fiction." In other words, it was useful to put the sun at the center for your calculations of where planetary positions should be.

People didn't believe heliocentrism was literally true, and most in fact didn't care because the main point of astronomy at the time was not to say something about the objective reality of the heavens, but rather to do calculations to say where the planets would be when so that you could use them for astrological predictions. In other words, the objective reality of celestial mechanics was just not important to them. They wanted the right answer and easy calculations.

Now to Galileo. In his early days, Galileo was not a Copernican, but by the start of the 17th century he had become convinced of Copernicus's hypothesis. He began arguing for it, using in part, some of the new telescopic findings that he had made, and in part by trying to develop a new physics that would be coherent with Copernican astronomy. One of the earliest hints of concern arose over breakfast in December 1613. Galileo wasn't present, but one of his students, and his successor as professor of mathematics at the University of Pisa, Father Benedetto Castelli, a Benedictine priest, was there. The breakfast was held at one of the palaces of Galileo's employer, the Dukes de' Medici in Florence. The Medici that was present there was the dowager duchess, Christina, mother of Cosimo II de' Medici, who was actually the ruling grand duke. She asked Castelli if Galileo's heliocentric ideas didn't contradict the Bible, particularly the Joshua story. As we learned from a letter Castelli immediately wrote to Galileo, the duchess did this as much out of pure curiosity as out of any kind of concern. Castelli answered as best he could, and as he says to Galileo, the duchess seems to have been quite satisfied.

Galileo wrote Castelli a letter in response, one which he would greatly expand into a letter addressed directly to the Grand Duchess Christina. In both letters, Galileo argued that scripture had to be interpreted in the light of scientific knowledge, and that its expressions were accommodated to the original audience. What does that mean? It means that, in fact, let's say the Joshua story was written from the point of view of the ancient Hebrew people who believed that the earth was stable and the sun was in motion around it. So the doctrine of accommodation says that the inspired writers thought it better not to confuse their original audience by telling them things they really didn't need to know or that conflicted with commonsense experience. It would have detracted from the main message. Remember what St. Thomas Aquinas says, that the scripture speaks according to the opinion of the people, that is, its original audience.

This should all sound very familiar from our lecture on St. Augustine. Galileo quoted the clever motto of a colleague, Cardinal Baronio, who said the Bible was to tell us how to go to heaven, not how the heavens go. But additionally, and perhaps injudiciously, as we shall see, Galileo went on to provide his own reinterpretation of the Joshua passage. He argued that the literal meaning could be saved owing to his recent discovery of the sun's rotational motion. Galileo theorized that since the sun rotated in the same direction that the planets revolved around it, that solar rotation was actually the cause for planetary motion. Therefore, he says, when scripture states that Joshua stopped the sun, it doesn't refer to the sun's apparent motion from east to west across the sky, but rather that rotation, which had been invisible until the time of Galileo. When the rotation was miraculously stopped, the rest of the solar system shut down simultaneously, including terrestrial rotation, thus making the sun appear to stand still and lengthening the day.

About a year later, on the fourth Sunday of Advent in 1614, the Dominican friar Tommaso Caccini preached a sermon at Santa Maria Novella in Florence. The Old Testament reading for the day was the Joshua passage. Caccini first expounded it in a moral and allegorical sense, but then went on to criticize Copernicus, mathematicians, and Galileo and his followers in particular. Some in attendance took umbrage at this and asked the usual homilist to preach a contrary sermon the next Sunday. In fact, Caccini's superior actually wrote a letter of apology to Galileo.

But our first question is why was Caccini so upset? Less than a month later, in February of 1615, another Florentine Dominican, Niccolò Lorini, wrote a letter of complaint to the Inquisition. He forwarded a copy of Galileo's letter to Castelli, saying that it contained suspect ideas. Now the Inquisition was a very orderly institution. It was not an anything-goes, out-of-control institution. In fact, reading Inquisition records, most people are struck by the attention to protocol, to due process, and to clarity. In their usual efficient way, the Inquisition examined the complaint. Galileo's letter was found to have what were called "bad expressions," that is, word choices that might be benign—probably were—but sounded bad.

For example, at one point, he says that Holy Scripture perverts certain things. But the consultant found no serious objections. Interestingly enough, two out of the three bad expressions occur only in the copy that Lorini sent to the Inquisition, not in Galileo's original. So this suggests that someone, maybe Lorini, was trying to make Galileo look bad. Where did this copy of the letter come from anyway? Well the Inquisition summoned Caccini. Caccini then claimed that Galileo and his followers hold seriously heretical views, for example, that God weeps and laughs and that the miracles of the saints are not true miracles. The Inquisition panel, which up to this point has seemed pretty bored by Caccini's mutterings, suddenly perks up and takes notice. They've heard something serious now.

On further questioning, Caccini admits that in fact he's only heard some rumors from, guess who, Lorini. Others are called in, and in the end, they interview one Giannozzo Attavanti, a minor cleric, and they find out what really was going on. Several months earlier, Attavanti, who knew Galileo but was no real close associate of his, was in the Dominican convent in Florence studying theology. He and his instructor were practicing a disputation. Scholastic disputations often work indirectly, like geometrical ones; you state the proposition as true that you're going to be refuting. So they said something like, "God laughs and cries;" therefore.... Somebody like Attavanti suggests, or as Attavanti suggests, must have been eavesdropping. The Inquisitors say, "Why would you think someone was eavesdropping? Who?" Attavanti replies that a few weeks previously, he had been discussing the question of the sun's motion, and some friar skulking about in the corridor burst in on them. "Ah ha! I hear what you're talking about." Who was the skulking friar? Tommaso Caccini. He sputtered at them for a few minutes and vowed to preach a sermon against the sun's motion, which, as we've seen, he did. Reading the minutes, you can almost see the Inquisitorial panel rolling its eyes at this discovery, and they dismissed the case.

All except, unfortunately, one little piece. They decide that they have no expertise to examine the status of heliocentrism. So what do they do? They do what any big administration does, they outsource to consultants. After four months of work, on the 24th of February in 1616—so this has been going on for a year now—the consultants turn in the report. It's damning. They conclude that Copernicanism is "foolish and absurd" in philosophy and "heretical" in theology. But then something curious happened. The Inquisition ignored the report. They could have declared Copernicanism heretical, but they didn't. Instead, they did two milder things. First, they turned to the Office of the Index, that is, the body that's charged with reviewing books and censoring them where necessary.

The Index then decreed that Copernicus's book was "suspended until corrected." What does that mean? It doesn't mean that Copernicus's text was prohibited or was to be destroyed; it means only that certain corrections should be made to it. It actually took four years before the corrections were published, indicating that this was not something high on the priority list. When they actually appeared, there were about 10 passages to be amended out of the entire book, all of them because they were offering interpretations of scripture or asserting straightforwardly that heliocentrism was absolutely true.

The second action was that Cardinal Roberto Bellarmino, one of the most powerful churchmen of the day in Rome and an important theologian, was told to meet with Galileo and inform him of the decree of the Index and also to give him a verbal warning to abandon his opinions about Copernicanism being literally true. This meeting happened in February 1616. Unfortunately, what exactly happened at that meeting would become a subject of controversy. All we know is Bellarmino gave a warning; Galileo agreed.

Now let's examine these events. What's clear first of all is that Caccini and Lorini, two minor friars in Florence, had some kind of beef with Galileo. Galileo was particularly acid-tongued and never suffered fools gladly. So perhaps there was some kind of personal affront here. Perhaps they were just overzealous, either legitimately so or in the typical kind of way that various low-order functionaries, whether in church, in business, or in academe, looking for advancement, tend to be. We don't know. However it started, the whole affair took on a life of its own with the decree of the Index—that's the crucial moment. Clearly, there was dissension within the Inquisition, since they ignored the panel's recommendation to condemn heliocentrism.

Bellarmino is really the most interesting character. Let's look at him a little more. The best source is a letter that Bellarmino wrote to a Neapolitan priest named Paolo Antonio Foscarini in 1615, just while all this was going on. In that year, Foscarini published a book reinterpreting the Bible to be compatible with Copernicanism, and he sent a copy to

Bellarmino. Foscarini probably was aware of the goings-on in Rome about heliocentrism and thought he would weigh in on them. Bellarmino's reply is very revealing. Bellarmino praises Foscarini and Galileo by name for speaking "suppositionally and not absolutely" about their theories for—and let me quote Bellarmino's letter:

> There is no danger in saying that by assuming the earth moves and the sun stands still, one saves all the appearances better than by postulating eccentrics and epicycles [as in the old Ptolemaic system], and that is sufficient for the mathematician. However, it is different to want to affirm that in reality, the sun is at the center of the world and the earth revolves with great speed around it. This is a very dangerous thing, likely not only to irritate all scholastic philosophers and theologians, but also to harm the holy faith by rendering Holy Scripture false.

In other words, heliocentrism is fine as a hypothesis, but don't demand that it's a true depiction of the cosmos.

Bellarmino further claims that if there were an undeniable demonstration of the earth's motion, then scripture would have to be reinterpreted carefully in accord with this new finding. But, he says, he will not believe there is such a demonstration until it is shown to me. Galileo himself must have gotten a copy of Bellarmino's letter. He'd gone to Rome at this time, and he knew Bellarmino personally, and he wrote a short rebuttal to it. The last piece we need to know is that when the Index suspended Copernicus's book, it condemned Foscarini's.

Now we see that biblical interpretation is a key issue here, but not in an entirely straightforward way. Let's start with Galileo's letters to Castelli and Christina. Galileo's writings show an exemplary understanding of accepted principles of biblical exegesis. Some parts seem to be taken verbatim out of St. Augustine. He lists the unity of truth, the doctrine of accommodation, and uses a style of literal interpretation that the African doctor would certainly have approved of. Galileo's theological principles are sound and orthodox.

Furthermore, earlier writers had already discussed the possibility of the earth's motion, and it reinterpreted the Joshua passage without incident. Already 250 years earlier, two masters at Paris, Jean Buridan and Nicole Oresme, had separately proposed arguments for a moving earth. Both eventually settled against it, but the point is that there was no great tumult after they made these proposals. What they did, in fact, is decided that you really can't tell the distinction between a moving earth and a moving sun because they are in relative motion, and we're part of the system and there's no test you can do. So they fell back on commonsense experience that the earth seems stable.

My point is that given Galileo's good grasp of exegesis and the previous lack of problems with similar discussions, it would seem that there's something special about Galileo and his time. We don't have to look far to find it—the Protestant Reformation. The Reformation, less than 100 years old in Galileo's day and still spreading, had thrown the Catholic Church into confusion. One result was the Council of Trent, a church council that met for 18 years, from 1545 to 1563. The point of the council was to clarify Catholic doctrine and practice and to address certain abuses that had been criticized by Protestants.

A main cause for the continuing schisms, which is a thing that the Council of Trent was very concerned about, was the daily emergence of novel and often unlearned interpretations of scripture that had the effect of undermining long-established theological positions; even Luther eventually was appalled by this trend. Protestant thinkers emphasized the notion of personal interpretation of scripture, so the Council of Trent—where Bellarmino by the way was a key figure— forbade the reinterpretation of scripture in ways "contrary to the consensus of the church fathers," that is, the Patristic writers. In other words, if you're giving an interpretation, it should conform to the traditional readings expressed by early writers.

So when Galileo and Foscarini wrote, it was in an atmosphere that was hypercharged with concern, we can say even paranoid about nonstandard biblical interpretations. Clearly, both Galileo and Foscarini violated the ruling of the Council of Trent. Obviously no Patristic writer would have ever thought of getting heliocentrism out of the Joshua passage. But remember, Copernicus himself reinterpreted scripture without immediate repercussions. But that was 1543, before the Council of Trent.

Galileo probably added some fuel to the fire though, for in his letter to Christina, he violates intellectual turf a little. He claims that his biblical interpretations are not just alternative, but they are better than the theologians' interpretations. Moreover, he tells theologians to stay out of natural philosophy, a sort of "Well you can't do my job, but I can do your job better." We all know people like this, and they are never very popular.

Notice that Bellarmino did not rule out the possibility that scriptural interpretation would have to be amended in the light of new demonstrated truths. In this, he, like Galileo, was adhering to the principles annunciated by St. Augustine. But Bellarmino required a sound demonstration of the earth's motion. And once that was found, then the proper authorities—not some mathematician from Florence—would go about carefully to expound a new and improved interpretation. So you can see here that the issue of biblical interpretation is linked to how much proof there really is for a moving earth, the validity of Galileo's proofs.

Bellarmino and Galileo agree on fundamental Augustinian principles. Their difference was the level of proof needed before reinterpretation kicked in, and who exactly would be doing the reinterpretation. Galileo claimed he had a proof. Bellarmino denied this. In this case, Bellarmino was right. Galileo advanced two telescopic proofs. He discovered first that the planet Venus showed phases like the moon. This would be impossible unless Venus orbited the sun and passed at some point between us, the Earth, and the sun. In Ptolemy's system this is impossible. But while it does disprove Ptolemy system, it doesn't prove Copernicus's. In fact, Galileo's observations are perfectly well explained by other geocentric models, like that of Tycho Brahe, or the 5th-century system of Martianus Capella where Mercury and Venus go around the sun but then that combination goes around the Earth.

Galileo also pointed to his discovery of the satellites of Jupiter. They proved that orbital motion could take place around some center of motion that wasn't at the center, that wasn't the earth, that wasn't the sun. That's great, but it doesn't prove that the earth goes around the sun. But Galileo's favorite proof was that the tides are caused by the motion of the earth. It's completely wrong. So while Galileo was ultimately correct about heliocentrism, he was wrong to think that he had proof.

We naturally enough look at things from Galileo's perspective. Look at them for a moment from Bellarmino's. Imagine the utter confusion that would result if the scriptures had to be reinterpreted for every possible unproven scientific system. Bellarmino was holding out for a sound proof, and Galileo just didn't have it. The interesting point is that Galileo and Bellarmino were in substantial agreement about harmonizing biblical interpretations with scientific knowledge. Where they differed was on who would do the reinterpretation and when. Bellarmino was cautious, more cautious than Galileo's enthusiasm would allow.

But there may have been other factors as well. Galileo might have been caught in a power struggle between rival intellectual elites within the church. Since the late Middle Ages, it was the Dominicans that had been on the top of the intellectual heap. In Galileo's day, they were rapidly being replaced by the Jesuits. In fact, some Jesuit schools, which were popping up all over Europe by the late 16th century, were even starting to teach about Copernicanism. Remember, Galileo's accusers, Lorini and Caccini, were Dominicans. And the majority of the consultants that returned the bad verdict on Copernicanism were Dominicans as well. Galileo, although he had run-ins with the Jesuits, like he did with essentially everybody, was for the most part on good terms with them. The Jesuits had welcomed him to their institution in Rome, the Collegio Romano, and when they were requested to do so, they verified his telescopic observations, although they denied his interpretations.

Even if this explanation turns out to be not so important, it points out an important caveat. We are not free to indulge in collectivism; that is, extending the actions of specific churchmen into a generalized statement about Galileo versus "the church," much less about science versus religion. There were clergy, theologians, and officials on both sides of the issue.

We now have to consider the events that followed Bellarmino's meeting with Galileo. Less than a week after the decree of the Index, Galileo went to see the pope. Unfortunately, there is obviously no transcript of their private meeting, but we do have Galileo's account of it. Galileo was warmly received, and he and the pope talked for about 45 minutes. The pope acknowledged that Galileo had certain enemies, but stated that both he and the cardinals thought very well of him and that they would not give ear to certain unnamed slanderers, so Galileo could, in the pope's words, "feel safe as long as I live." This would prove not quite long enough.

Then Galileo heard that rumors about his having been condemned were circulating. To defend his reputation, he went to visit

Bellarmino again and asked for a certificate setting out exactly what had happened. Bellarmino agreed and gave Galileo a certificate stating clearly that Galileo had not abjured anything, nor had he been condemned, nor had he been punished in any way, but had only been informed of the decree of the Index about Copernicus's book needing correction and informed that he should not hold or defend Copernicanism. This certificate would prove crucial later on.

So at the end of the first act of the Galileo affair, March 1616, Galileo headed home to Florence, having been asked privately not to defend the Copernican hypothesis as literally true. The only public sign of the events was that the Index had suspended Copernicus's book until corrected.

In the next lecture, we will see what happened when Galileo received what he thought was great good news in 1623.

Lecture Six
Galileo's Trial

Scope:

After more than 15 years of calm, Galileo got into trouble in 1632–1633 because of his book *Dialogue on the Two Chief World Systems.* In the end, he abjured the motion of the Earth as a false doctrine and spent the rest of his life under house arrest. This lecture examines this latter phase of the Galileo affair, presents explanations of the events, and looks at how these events have been used, abused, and reexamined down to the present day. Of particular importance are the arguments made on both sides about the relative intellectual roles of science and faith and the levels of certainty we can have about each.

Outline

I.   In 1623, Galileo's friend and admirer Maffeo Barberini was elected Pope Urban VIII.

　　A. Galileo soon thereafter published *Il Saggiatore*, dedicating it to the new pope. Some charges were made against the book regarding its implications for the Eucharist, but the Inquisition dismissed these as groundless.

　　B. In early 1624, Galileo went to Rome and met with the pope; he was warmly received.

　　　　1. They discussed the Earth's motion, and the pope said that Galileo could write about it, provided that he included one particular epistemological argument.

　　　　2. This argument was Urban VIII's contention that because God is omnipotent, the determination of ultimate causes can never be absolutely certain; that is, a given phenomenon could have various causes.

　　　　3. The pope was later heard to say that the Index's decree should have been prevented.

　　C. Galileo set to work, first writing a (sarcastic) reply to Francesco Ingoli, who had written against the Earth's motion in 1616.

　　D. He then began a dialogue, first entitled *On the Tides* but later called *A Dialogue on the Two Chief World Systems.*

　　　　1. The events surrounding its publication were tortuous.

2. In 1630, Galileo went to Rome to print the book; he received approval from Niccolò Riccardi, Vatican secretary and chief censor.
3. Problems (death, plague, and delays) intervened, and Galileo moved to publish the work in Florence. The secretary sent a list of alterations and transferred authority to publish to Florence.
4. The book was finally published in 1632.

II. Although the book was widely praised, questions and rumors arose at Rome, initiating the final phase of the Galileo affair.
   A. Pope Urban VIII was furious with Galileo: "I have been deceived!"
      1. Galileo put the pope's argument only on the last page of the book and into the mouth of a fool.
      2. The pope learned for the first time of Galileo's 1616 agreement with Bellarmino—something Galileo "forgot to mention."
   B. In terms of "external factors," the pope was under duress at this time owing to the Thirty Years' War, which he refused to support. His secretary, who continued to voice his support of Galileo to the pope, also supported the Spanish party that was trying to depose Urban.
   C. Galileo was summoned to Rome and questioned.
      1. The Inquisitors produced a document from 1616, in which Galileo agreed not to discuss Copernicanism.
      2. Galileo was surprised by the document, which did not bear his signature. He presented Bellarmino's certificate, which in turn, surprised the Inquisitors.
   D. The legal case was very specific—it was not about heliocentrism—rather, did Galileo violate the terms of his 1616 agreement with Bellarmino?
      1. Galileo argued that he didn't really believe heliocentrism was true but was just playing around to make a weak argument look strong.
      2. A lenient "plea bargain" was reached.
      3. But Pope Urban VIII dismissed the bargain and ordered a formal trial; Galileo was convicted in June 1633 of "vehement suspicion of heresy," and he abjured the Earth's motion.

E. Francesco Barberini, the pope's nephew, did not sign the conviction—nor did two other cardinals—a possible signal that it was, in part, the result of a "show trial."

III. Significant philosophical issues were involved throughout the case.

   A. A key issue is the split between realist and instrumentalist views of science.

   B. Realism holds that scientific theories are *true* depictions of the world.

   C. Instrumentalism holds that scientific theories are simply *tools* for providing plausible explanations and for "saving the phenomena."

   D. Superimposed on the Galileo affair was a contemporaneous shift in astronomy from instrumentalism to realism.

   E. Copernicus, Kepler, Galileo (and most modern scientists) are realists; Bellarmino, Urban VIII, the Collegio Romano, and probably most practicing astronomers of the day were instrumentalists.

   F. Copernicus's book likewise shows this tension in the unsigned preface added to it (without Copernicus's knowledge) by the Lutheran minister Andreas Osiander.

   G. The realist position—although characteristic of modern science—is ultimately a choice and a faith statement (one that facilitates modern research).

IV. In 1979, Pope John Paul II convened a commission to reinvestigate Galileo's case. Besides an admission of "errors committed," the report contained a reaffirmation of Augustinian principles of exegesis (as upheld by Galileo) and the ultimate compatibility of faith and reason.

Essential Reading:

Finocchiaro, *The Galileo Affair*, pp. 200–202 (correction to Copernicus), 204–226, 227–293.

Supplementary Reading:

Finocchiaro, *The Galileo Affair*, pp. 154–197.

Lindberg and Numbers, *God and Nature*, chapter 3 (pp. 76–113).

Questions to Consider:

1. If you were Galileo, how might you have handled things differently? What if you were Bellarmino or Urban VIII?

2. The philosophical and intellectual differences between Galileo and Urban VIII center on human abilities to acquire sure knowledge of causation (remember Lecture Four?). Can you suggest any rational method for resolving the difference between them? Any pragmatic method?

Lecture Six—Transcript
Galileo's Trial

In the last lecture, we left Galileo on his way home to Florence in spring 1616. For the next seven years, Galileo busied himself with matters other than Copernicanism. But in August 1623, shortly after the death of Pope Paul V, Galileo received what he thought was wonderful news. His old friend and admirer, Maffeo Barberini, had been elected pope, taking the name Urban VIII. Galileo was then finishing a book entitled *Il Saggiatore*, or *The Assayer*, which dealt with a broad range of issues. Galileo took the opportunity to dedicate his new book to the pope, who was delighted with it, but the Inquisition soon received a complaint about it. The Inquisition investigated; they weren't convinced by the complaint at all and dismissed it as groundless, and Galileo probably never knew about it.

In early 1624, Galileo traveled to Rome to visit Pope Urban VIII. He was warmly received by his old friend in not one, but six separate audiences over several days. Of course, since these were private conversations, we don't have minutes to them, unfortunately, but it's clear that they discussed the old issue of the earth's motion. Urban VIII now had been one of Galileo's advocates back in 1616 and was later heard to say that the decree of the Index suspending Copernicus' book should have been prevented.

During their discussions, the pope apparently gave Galileo the go-ahead to write about the Copernican hypothesis, provided that he did so in a hypothetical manner and included one particular argument. This was Urban VIII's contention that since God is omnipotent, the determination of ultimate causes can never be absolutely certain; that is, a given phenomenon could be generated by more than a single cause and still appear identical to our eyes. You should recognize this as something we've talked about previously, namely, God's activity in the world and the discernment of miracles. How can we really reliably get at the true causes of things?

Urban's argument is that, given divine omnipotence, God could have created the world in any number of different ways, in ways where the causes are different, even though the effects we witness are the same. Thus, while Galileo was certain, and completely wrong, that the tides were caused by the motion of the earth, in a sense the way water sloshes around in a container that's in motion, the pope was more skeptical, or at least more cautious, and argued that the tides might have another cause. In fact, it might even be a cause that we would never think of.

Well, as soon as Galileo got back to Florence, he set to work. First, he wrote a reply to Francesco Ingoli's critique of the Copernican system. Ingoli was a minor cleric, also a minor critic, in fact, who had written against the earth's motion in 1616 when the Inquisition's consultants were weighing the issue. Remember, the panel decided that Copernicanism was heretical, but the Inquisition took no action in this.

If you have a chance to read Galileo's reply to Ingoli, you will see that some warning signs are already apparent. While Ingoli's arguments are in fact quite feeble, even silly, Galileo's reply lashes out at several points with bitter sarcasm and indeed a bit of arrogance. Galileo was a brilliant writer, absolutely a wonderful writer, of Italian prose. But when that talent was combined with his inability to suffer lesser wits and his delight in arguing, even to the point of being contrarian at some times, it produced a personality that created more enemies than he really needed. Eventually, the same trait would alienate an old, and now very powerful, friend.

So Galileo then began writing a dialogue. He entitled it simply *On the Tides* because it showcased his argument that the tides prove the motion of the earth. By 1630, the manuscript was ready. The events surrounding its publication, however, are just as torturous as the rest of the Galileo affair. Galileo wanted to print it at Rome under the auspices of the Lyncean Academy, the first international scientific society, which was headed by his friend, Prince Federico Cesi. So Galileo packed up his manuscript and headed to Rome in May 1630. He submitted it to review to the Vatican secretary and chief censor for publications in Rome, Niccolò Riccardi.

After a few weeks, he received approval to go ahead with the printing after he had made some finishing touches and had made a final check with Riccardi. So Galileo left Rome with the impression that the publication of his book was going forward, but problems immediately intervened. Before printing could start, Cesi died. Without a patron, the Lyncean Academy collapsed. Then plague broke out in central Italy, interrupting all travel in commerce between Florence and Rome. Galileo could neither travel to Rome nor send his manuscript in for the final check because it would have been quarantined at the border.

By March 1631, Galileo lost patience and moved to have the book published in Florence instead. But this caused new problems. The book had been cleared for publication in Rome after a final check by the Roman censor, but the Roman censor's authority didn't extend to Florence. So, much of the summer of 1632 involved negotiations to transfer the permission to publish from Rome to Florence. Riccardi, in due course, affected the transfer and sent along a list of alterations that Galileo was to address. It is at this time that the title of the book was changed from *On the Tides* to *A Dialogue on the Two Chief World Systems*, a suggestion which supposedly came from the pope himself.

Ironically enough, this change had the unintended effect of making Galileo's book much more influential than it otherwise might have been. It moved Galileo's error about the tides out of the limelight and replaced it with a broader comparison of the Ptolemaic and Copernican systems, which of course is what Galileo got right.

Anybody who has gone through the process of publishing a book or paper will find very little in this process that's terribly unusual. Of course, today one would not be expected to make changes to a scientific manuscript based on potential theological problems or consequences, but that's not really the point I am trying to make. I point out only that modern sensibilities, when they heard the word "censor," recoil. We think immediately of the old Soviet Union or modern-day China or some other repressive totalitarian regime. But in fact, a manuscript today still has to pass muster with reviewers. They are not called censors anymore, but their role is really not terribly different.

Every academic has had a paper refused for publication or a manuscript held up for years awaiting publication. Publishers routinely require that titles be changed or that specific passages be altered or amended before publication. It would be easy to retort that nowadays this is peer review; it's not the interference by some meddling churchmen, but that again, in part, is a modernism that sees churchmen residing in a class that's separate from scientists or natural philosophers. In fact, Riccardi sent Galileo's manuscript to a professor of mathematics who was also a churchman. Galileo's book was finally published in Florence in February of 1632. The book received immediate praise, but rumors about it started to arise just as immediately. And here begins the second phase of the Galileo affair.

Remember that the pope was an old friend of Galileo's. So one might expect that the rumors and complaints that arise could have been fairly easily stopped by the pope himself. My guess is that Galileo counted on this. That's not what happened, however. In fact, the opposite happened. Urban VIII exploded in anger at Galileo. Why? There were a number of factors. First of all, I think we have to explain the pope's repeated declarations to the Tuscan ambassador that, "I have been deceived." What did he mean by this?

There were probably two injudicious moves on Galileo's part. The first one deals with his discharge of the pope's request to include the argument about the limits of human knowledge in the dialogue. Galileo did include it, but how he did so was certainly enough to infuriate Urban VIII. Galileo wrote the book as a dialogue between three characters. The first, by the name of Salviati, speaks for the Copernican system and is really Galileo's mouthpiece. His opponent speaks for Aristotelian physics and Ptolemaic cosmology and is named Simplicio. The third, Sagredo, is the impartial intermediary who asks questions. The name "Simplicio" could refer to the 5th-century Aristotelian commentator, Simplicius. But any Italian reader would immediately see the pun on the words "simple" and "simpleton." And indeed, poor Simplicio is cast as a gibbering idiot time and time again throughout the dialogue. So where do you think Galileo puts the pope's argument? On the very last page of the book and in the mouth of Simplicio.

Even if Galileo didn't want to put it in the mouth of his own spokesman, Salviati, he could have given the line to Sagredo, but he chose Simplicio. Simplicio's closing utterance is this: "God in his infinite power and wisdom could have conferred upon the element of water the back-and-forth motion that we see in it by some other means than by making its container move." Urban's words from the mouth of the fool, and they are greeted with a response that could easily be read as sarcastic, "What a marvelous and truly angelic doctrine." If that's a sincere compliment, it's the only one that Simplicio ever gets in the dialogue.

And secondly, somebody looked into the old Inquisition files back from 1616 and found that Galileo had agreed not to defend the Copernican system. Galileo had neglected to mention this to the pope, who knew nothing about it. The panel that examined the case of Galileo concluded that Galileo, "May have been deceitfully silent about this injunction." So I think it's fairly easy to understand why Urban VIII felt that he had been betrayed by his friend. Urban had supported and protected Galileo. He had even written a poem in his honor. He had given him the go-ahead to write the dialogue and here was his reward—embarrassment and insult.

Urban might have eventually forgiven Galileo, but there were aggravating circumstances. In short, this problem was the last thing that Urban VIII needed in 1632. The pope was having a very bad year. He was under heavy criticism for his response to the Thirty Years' War, and there was a movement afoot to depose him. The Thirty Years' War was a disastrous conflict in Germany over territory and dynastic claims wrapped up in the mantel of Catholic-Protestant conflict. On one side were the Catholic powers of the Holy Roman Emperor and the King of Spain, both of them part of the Hapsburg dynasty. On the other was a group of Protestant German states and Sweden, who by the way were being bankrolled by the most Catholic King of France, who had every reason to want to see the Hapsburg powers worn down.

In 1632, the war was going very badly for emperor and Spain. While the pope was sending his nephew to France to try to hammer out a peace treaty, the emperor and Spain demanded that the pope intervene on their side with money and forces or, at the very least, declare the conflict a holy war. Urban refused. The result was that the Spanish party rallied against Urban with threats of impeachment, accusations of weakness as a leader, and even rumors that he was in fact in league with the Protestants. Put yourself in Urban's red shoes for a moment. You are under attack, your reputation, honor, and position in jeopardy, and now along comes your friend with what has every appearance of deception and embarrasses you at a delicate, intense moment when your attention has to be elsewhere. Thus, Urban VIII, rather than sweeping in to help Galileo, let matters take their course and seemed intent on making an example of him.

Galileo was summoned for questioning. He first pleaded his age—he was 68—and the difficulty of travel, but these were rejected, and he had to go to Rome in January of 1633. Now from time to time, fictionalized accounts of Galileo in chains in an inquisitorial dungeon have emerged. In fact, Galileo was very well treated. He might have had some enemies; he might have alienated the pope, but he still had lots of admirers and friends in church circles. He was neither arrested nor imprisoned at this point. He stayed in the palace of the Tuscan ambassador.

In April 1633, he was summoned for questioning. At this point, the Inquisitors showed him a document from 1616 where he agreed not to discuss Copernicanism in any way whatsoever. In other words, Galileo had been given a special injunction not to do exactly what he did. Galileo was surprised. He claimed only that he had been given a warning by Bellarmino and presented the Inquisitors with Bellarmino's certificate. In turn, the Inquisitors were surprised because they had never known anything about this certificate either. Its language is milder than the document that was found in the Inquisition files. Indeed, there's something a little fishy about that document that was found in the Inquisition files because it should have borne Galileo's and Bellarmino's signatures, but it's unsigned.

Scholars still debate the origin of this document. Was it a sloppy record from 1616? Was it the fabrication of some overzealous functionary? Was there just a misunderstanding on one side or the other of what Galileo and Bellarmino had agreed to? Probably we'll never know the answer, and neither could the Inquisition because the only person who could have resolved it, Bellarmino himself, was dead.

At this point, the case turned to a very specific legal matter. It was not about heliocentrism, rather the question that the Inquisitors had was simple—in writing the dialogue, did Galileo violate his 1616 agreement with Bellarmino? Galileo was asked specifically why he didn't get written permission to write the book in the first place, why he didn't mention Bellarmino's warning to the pope? Well, Galileo's response seems rather unsatisfactory. He claimed that he never imagined his book was actually defending heliocentrism, so he thought that Bellarmino's warning was not relevant. Galileo stated moreover that he didn't really think that heliocentrism was true anyway; he was just playing around trying to make a weak argument look strong. "Maybe…" he says, "I overdid it." This seems a big stretch. But the Inquisitors seemed to accept it.

What the Inquisitors did next will be absolutely familiar to anyone who has seen a few episodes of *Law and Order*. They propose a plea bargain to avoid going to trial. The deal was this: Galileo would admit to having inadvertently broken his agreement. Galileo took a few days to come up with an honorable way of saying this, and finally he claimed that he was actually surprised when he reread his own book because, my goodness, it did sound like he was defending geokinetic theory even though that was far from his mind. He had just written a little too vividly, and he regretted it.

That should have been the end of it. Ordinarily, the pope would have rubberstamped the Inquisition's actions. But in this case, the pope refused to accept the settlement. Instead, he demanded Galileo had to be formally arrested, formally interrogated and sentenced, and he had to make a public abjuration, and his book had to be banned. The far gentler measures that the Inquisition had worked out, which would have sent Galileo home with essentially a slap on the wrist and his honor intact, were thrown out.

In grim order, Galileo was arrested and formally interrogated on the 21st of June in 1633. He stuck to his story about never really holding Copernican ideas, but was convicted of "vehement suspicion of heresy," the middle level of three levels of sentences the Inquisition could issue. The following day, he was read the sentence and recited a formal abjuration. He did not, as some romantic writers have suggested, mutter *Eppur si muove*, "and yet it moves," under his breath. Cute story, not true.

In all regards, Galileo, rather uncharacteristically, acted with humility and submission. But there's one more oddity: Galileo's sentence should have been signed by all ten of the Inquisitors, but three of them didn't sign. One was the head of the Spanish Party, then trying to oust the pope, further indicating that there was some kind of link between these two issues. It also bears witness to the close relationship between the Duke of Tuscany—Galileo's employer—and the Spanish. This Spanish-Tuscan link provides another possible reason why Urban VIII might have wanted to embarrass the Tuscan duke by embarrassing his court philosopher and banning the dialogue that bore the duke's name in large letters on the title page.

But another Cardinal who didn't sign is more interesting. It was Francesco Barberini, the pope's nephew and the most powerful man in Rome after the pope. Perhaps we can read into this a very Roman way of indicating quietly that the trial was really for show, that Urban really didn't endorse it.

Galileo returned to the Tuscan embassy, then to the home of the Archbishop of Siena, one of his friends and supporters, and then retired to his villa at Arcetri outside of Florence, where he remained under house arrest for the rest of his life. As we've seen, there were several external factors that impacted on the Galileo affair, but there's a further intellectual issue we have to address. It opens a window onto some assumptions of modern science that were just being developed in the 17th century. What I refer to is the split between a realist and an instrumentalist view of science. What do those terms mean? Realism holds that scientific theories are true depictions of the world; scientific ideas really do describe the world as it objectively is.

Instrumentalism, on the other hand, holds that scientific theories are simply useful tools for saving the phenomenon. What does saving the phenomena actually mean? It means that if we see some set of phenomena, say the various motions of the heavenly bodies and planets, the sun and moon, then the goal of science is simply to propose a coherent model for explaining and predicting these phenomena. Whether or not the theory is literally true of objective reality behind the observable phenomena is irrelevant. We get a better handle on the Galileo affair when we recognize that superimposed on it was a contemporaneous shift within astronomy from instrumentalism to realism. Most modern scientists are realists. They expect the scientific theories they elaborate to be accurate, true depictions of the way the world really is.

They are joined in this conviction by Nicholas Copernicus, Johannes Kepler, and Galileo Galilee. Indeed, Kepler and Galileo were emphatic about their desire to give fully real—that is true—descriptions of the hidden mechanisms behind the visible movements of the planets. This sounds absolutely normal to us today, but for their immediate audience, it was really quite unusual. Most practicing astronomers of their day were instrumentalists, as had been the case since the ancient Greeks. Their interest was getting planetary positions right, being able to calculate what planet would be where when, in past, present, or future. Why would they really care about what was really going on mechanically in the heavens if it didn't make a visible difference to the phenomena? In short, why bend yourself out of shape over arguing Copernican versus Ptolemaic system if it didn't give you a different answer?

We saw how some astronomers adopted a Copernican system to make calculations easier, without thinking that Copernicus's system was any truer than Ptolemy's. In terms of the characters around

Galileo, Bellarmino, Urban VIII, and many of the Jesuit astronomers of the Collegio Romano held the then majority instrumentalist opinion. So these characters kept telling Galileo just to discuss Copernicanism hypothetically.

In saying this, they probably had in mind the theological term *ex suppositione*, by supposition, meaning that you take a position suppositionally for the sake of the argument and see where it leads. I emphasize this point for two reasons: first, to say something about the changing nature of science. Don't imagine that it's static or predetermined. Even something as fundamental as the status of theories has to be worked out historically. Galileo was in the vanguard of scientific realists. But secondly, when we hear Bellarmino and Urban telling Galileo just to speak hypothetically, our modern ears tend to think this a little bit strange, or even that maybe it's some subtle way of shutting him up. But I would wager that Bellarmino and Urban were actually a bit confused by Galileo's fixation on claiming the literal truth for his notions.

Copernicus's own book shows the same tensions. Copernicus was a realist, but the Lutheran minister, Andreas Osiander, to whom the book had been entrusted to see it through the press, added an unsigned preface without Copernicus's knowledge, committing Copernicus to instrumentalism. Osiander wrote in this unsigned preface that he had published with *De revolutionibus* that, "The job of the astronomer is simply to think up whatever causes and hypotheses he pleases so that the movements of the planets can be calculated from the principles of geometry. For he cannot, by any line of reasoning, reach the true causes of these movements. Let no one expect anything certain from astronomy."

The realist position characteristic of modern science is ultimately a choice based on an optimistic faith statement, namely, that the human intellect can ascertain true causes, and we can work backwards from observables to true causes and recognize them as such. It's a question of values and aims. We have decided that science is supposed to get at true causes and not rest content with just workable accounts useful for prediction and explanation, but which do not make claims to objective truth. Science would not be as we know it today without these characteristics. But these are ultimately choices we make about how science is going to be.

In practice, scientists—most scientists at least—don't generally follow the realist road all the way to the end. I will give you an example. When I teach chemistry to my students, I use principles borrowed from physics to explain things at a fundamental level. Do I care whether these conceptions, these theories of physics, are true or not? I couldn't care less. They satisfy me; they satisfy my students by at least seeming to explain the things that we see in chemistry, and they explain things well enough to get us going towards what we really care about—chemistry. So I might be a realist about chemistry, but an instrumentalist when I borrow explanations from physics. Engineers often don't care about true causes so long as the theories they are using work to a successful, practical result, like using Ptolemaic astronomy to get correct planetary positions.

Philosophically speaking, we cannot really ever tell that we have uncovered true causes or even that we are able to uncover them. In this sense, Urban VIII and Bellarmino were right. But modern science does one of two things: either it gladly makes the leap of faith to assert that human beings can ascertain true causes, or it simply assumes that we can in order to get the rest of science off the ground and functioning. Having made that assumption, modern science has been pretty darn successful, hasn't it? Of course, it has. On the other hand, the argument from success is not an argument for objective truth of the starting assumption, only a verification that the assumption is working; that it is a good one.

In conclusion, a little epilogue. In 1979, only about a year into his pontificate, John Paul II made a widely publicized address to the Pontifical Academy of Sciences. He convened a commission to reopen Galileo's case. Having said that Galileo was made to suffer unnecessarily by one of his predecessors, he invited scientists, historians, and theologians to participate in this commission. The commission's final report takes notes of errors that were committed on both sides. Undoubtedly, chief among these on the church's side were the Index decree of 1616 and Urban's desire to make an example of Galileo in 1633. On Galileo's side, his rather less than forthright dealings with Urban VIII and his error about the tides.

More to the point, the report also contained a reaffirmation of Augustinian principles of exegesis as they were upheld in fact by Galileo. And it also referred to the ultimate compatibility of faith and reason, a topic we've already seen that was reiterated in the 1998 encyclical we mentioned previously.

So in sum, the Galileo affair includes a wide variety of issues that still command the attention of historians. In the past two lectures, I've tried to present a number of these issues, and I hope you can see how much we really lose if we allow ourselves to reduce this to a simple conflict of science and religion. In our next lecture, we are going to look at some conceptions of God and nature as they emerged in the 17th century.

Lecture Seven
God the Watchmaker

Scope:

The 17th-century introduction of the idea of a mechanical universe functioning like a great clockwork implied the creative actions of a divine mechanist but simultaneously distanced him from creation and could even make him seem unnecessary. Natural philosophers had to deal with this crisis, and their deep-seated fears over the new growth of irreligion and atheism provided a new context. This lecture surveys the problem and some of the means used to address it by Robert Boyle, Isaac Newton, and others, as well as the concomitant creation of a new problem: the "God of the gaps"—an unsatisfactory image of the deity wherein he is invoked as a cause for any problem for which science has no explanation, a sort of a scientific *deus ex machina*.

Outline

I. In the 17th century, a new conception of the natural world and its functioning was developed; it was called the *mechanical philosophy*.

   A. The mechanical philosophy conceived of the world as a great machine functioning mechanically; matter (generally composed of minute particles), its shape, and its motion explained all natural phenomena.

   B. This philosophy was proposed as a replacement to the Aristotelian natural philosophical system.

   C. Yet it also drew on notions of a *machina mundi* ("world machine") that had been developing since the Middle Ages.

   D. Some major proponents of this system were the priest Pierre Gassendi, René Descartes, Robert Boyle, and many others.

II. The theological impact of the mechanical philosophy was mixed.

   A. Gassendi, although he revived ancient atomism, insisted that the atoms were created and given their motion by God.

   B. The Minim priest Marin Mersenne seems to have advocated a mechanical system in order to buttress the doctrine of miracles and their discernibility.

C. The concept of the world as a machine or clockwork implied the existence of a divine craftsman; thus, it could be viewed as a support of religion. However, the *kind* of God it suggested was not necessarily orthodox; for example, it could suggest an "absentee God."

D. The mechanical philosophy also ran the risk of promoting materialism—the belief that matter is all there is (no spiritual entities).

    1. Concern over materialism continues to characterize intellectual theological responses down to the present.

    2. Materialism further invokes the danger of determinism—without entities external to matter and able to interact with it, then the motions of particles determine all future events, and there can be no free will.

    3. Materialism also almost unavoidably leads to atheism ("no spirits—no God").

    4. Fear of atheism was common in the late 17th century—this was, at the time, a new concern, but it has characterized religious (especially Protestant) apologetics and fears ever since.

III. Numerous responses to the mechanical philosophy were proposed to address its potential toward materialism, atheism, and other theologically unacceptable ideas.

A. Some thinkers, such as the Cambridge Platonists (including Henry More), argued that brute matter and motion were simply insufficient; they posited non-sentient, non-corporeal entities (the "spirit of nature" and the "plastic principle") to guide natural processes.

B. Robert Boyle (1627–1691) rejected this notion of the Cambridge Platonists, believing such entities to be unnecessary intermediaries between God and his creation.

    1. Boyle was deeply religious and viewed the role of the natural philosopher ("scientist") as a "priest of nature."

    2. This view of the study of the natural world as an inherently religious, devotional activity was common—it is linked to the concept of the Two Books.

    3. Boyle believed that God's activity was necessary to uphold the "common course of nature," because brute bodies cannot, of themselves, obey laws.

4. He attempted to defuse atheism and materialism by seeking authentic instances of spirit activity—in witchcraft and apparitions.

5. This was a widespread project in late-17th-century England, resulting partly from the loss of ecclesiastical recognition of miracles and, thus, of divine activity.

6. Boyle even brought his interest in alchemy (meaning the transmutation of metals into gold) in to help, because he believed that the philosophers' stone might be able to attract angels and facilitate communication with them.

7. What is key to recognize is that the investigation of spiritual phenomena was carried out by prominent natural philosophers; such studies could be as much a part of their investigations as chemistry or physics. This is no longer the case.

IV. One characteristic of the science-religion landscape of the 17th century was the conviction that scientific discoveries would provide the best support for religious belief.

A. The early Boyle Lectures—a series of lectures to combat atheism that began in 1692 and were funded in Boyle's will—offer revealing instances of this strategy.

B. The first Boyle lecturer was Richard Bentley (1662–1742); in eight lectures given in 1692, he used recent scientific discoveries to argue against atheism.

C. Much of the specific material Bentley used came from Sir Isaac Newton (1642–1727).

   1. Newton himself was deeply religious, as is the case (we must remember) for essentially *all* of the "scientific greats" of the early modern period.

   2. Newton's beliefs were, in fact, heretical, and he spent much time trying to identify and correct what he thought were "corruptions" in Scripture.

   3. Newton's *Principia mathematica* (1687), a foundational text of classical physics, freely discusses the attributes and activities of God.

   4. It was not unusual for physics texts of the time to deal with topics we today would consider "religious" and, thus, inappropriate for inclusion; this is evidence of the fluid (and culturally contingent) boundaries between science and religion over time.

5. Like many of his English contemporaries, Newton wanted to identify evidence of divine activity in the world; he may have believed gravity to be such activity.

D. Bentley's arguments use the structure of the Solar System as evidence of divine design and its continued stability as evidence of God's providence and continued activity.

E. But such arguments are problematic because they are an appeal to ignorance; they create an ultimately unsuitable "God of the gaps."

1. The phrase *God of the gaps* refers to an image of the deity (inadvertently) created by arguments that invoke his direct intercession to explain otherwise inexplicable phenomena or situations, that is, to "close the gaps" in otherwise naturalistic explanations.

2. But such gaps tend to close with the advance of scientific knowledge, thus putting religion in the position of constant retreat.

3. This is one background to the common belief (expressed by White) that religion always retreats before science. But such "retreat" is historically contingent—it depends on the choice to create and to rely on God-of-the-gaps arguments.

4. It is possible that some gaps cannot be closed, but historically speaking, these are few in comparison to the many proposed since the 17th century.

F. The use of knowledge of the natural world to support religious belief developed extensively in the 18th and 19th centuries; it became known as *natural theology*.

Essential Reading:

Lindberg and Numbers, *God and Nature*, chapters 5–6 (pp. 136–192).

Supplementary Reading:

Lawrence M. Principe, *Aspiring Adept*, pp. 190–212 (on Boyle, alchemy, and angels).

Questions to Consider:

1. Analyze the problems (for Christianity) with the concept of an absentee God and of a God of the gaps. Are these similar sorts of problems? How are they the same and how are they different? To what larger concerns do the concerns over these conceptions of the deity relate?

2. What would be the reception today of a physics text that treated the immortality of the soul and God's attributes? Why were things different for Newton and Boyle? Would the modern reception be markedly different if the text adopted an explicitly theistic or an explicitly atheistic position? How defensible would the modern response be? On what grounds?

Lecture Seven—Transcript
God the Watchmaker

The 17th century was an exciting time for both the history of science and the history of religion. It was a time for the history of science when many long-held scientific theories and concepts were significantly amended or replaced; hence the period is called by many the Scientific Revolution. We already saw, in the last lecture, one major change to the world picture that occurred in the 17th century, namely, the replacement of the traditional Aristotelian-Ptolemaic cosmos with the newer Copernican-Keplerian cosmos.

But another important development, and one that's perhaps more profound and more far-reaching, was a new view of the way the world functioned. I am referring to the emergence of a philosophy of nature called the mechanical philosophy. We saw earlier how man's concept of God affects his concept of nature. In turn, man's concept of nature affects his conception of God.

The development of the mechanical philosophy brought with it changes to man's thinking about God's activity in the world and God's relationship to mankind. In this lecture, we are going to look at how the 17th-century mechanical philosophy and 17th-century Christian theology interacted.

The mechanical philosophy envisions the universe as an immensely complicated clockwork or machine. Seventeenth-century writers liked, in particular, the comparison to a clockwork. Hidden behind all the dials and hands of astronomical clocks of the period, which displayed everything from lunar and solar cycles to elaborate automata with dancing figures and crowing cocks and all sorts of ingenious devices, lay unseen gears and wheels and pulleys that were what was responsible, the direct causes, for the movements that delighted the viewers.

So 17th-century thinkers drew a comparison between the world and what was for them a technological wonder of the age—the astronomical clock—just as, say, the computer is in ours. In living organisms, the levers and pulleys were to be revealed by anatomy and the new microscope. Individual organs became mechanical devices—the heart, a pump, the kidneys, filters, and indeed the whole body, a mass of plumbing and rigging. Some thinkers went so far as to claim that animals were little more than automata.

But the mechanical philosophy also worked on a much more fundamental level. In every substance, lying beneath the surface that we can see, was a simpler kind of clockwork, that is, swarms of minute particles, called atoms by some, corpuscles by others. These minute parts were in constant motion and endowed with particular shapes. And it was their motions and their collisions and shapes which were responsible for the qualities and the changes that we perceive in material substances. Basically, it's a billiard ball-type universe in a strict mechanical philosophy.

But before I go any further, I should just point out, if you haven't noticed it, that we are back with the big issue of hidden causation. As with many scientific developments, the mechanical philosophy turned out to be a mixed bag for theology. Let's look at some examples. One major proponent and developer of the mechanical philosophy was Pierre Gassendi, a priest from the south of France, mostly active in the 1630s to the 1650s. Gassendi had a very difficult job ahead of him. He was trying to use an atomic and mechanical system to replace Aristotelian conceptions of nature that had been dominant since the 13th century and had been worked into Christian theology. The system he was trying to replace them with, this atomic system, had been rejected already in antiquity and was tainted with atheism. So he had a tough job.

But he made several changes to the ancient system of atomism. The ancient Greek Epicurus and his Roman popularizer, Lucretius, asserted that the atoms were infinite in number, eternal, and self-moving. Gassendi, on the other hand, said that the atoms were finite in number, they were created by God, and moreover, God had endowed them with their motion, thus introducing activity and change into the world. Gassendi additionally did a very important thing, that is, asserting the existence of the human soul as an immaterial substance, that is, something not composed of atoms. And he affirmed a belief in human free will, in accordance with Christian theology, of course.

Thus Gassendi Christianized ancient atomism and incorporated it into a mechanical view of nature. Well, while Gassendi worried about Christianizing atomic mechanism, at about the same time another Frenchman actually adopted the mechanical philosophy precisely because of the benefits he thought it held out for Christian theology. The Minim priest, Marin Mersenne, was the Internet of his age. He created a network of correspondence all across Europe facilitating the exchange of ideas and letters between all sorts of different people. This kind of position, later called an intelligencer, became crucial in the 17th century for the exchange of ideas in international networks. Mersenne now seems to have advocated a mechanical system in the doctrine of miracles. How?

If the world functions by the motions and collisions of minute particles, then the emergence of phenomena in nature must be perfectly regular. In other words, you have in the mechanical philosophy a comprehensive explanation for all phenomena; so, determining that *cursus communis naturae*, that common course of nature, will be much easier, more exact. And once you've done that, miracles will stick out like a sore thumb. They will be easy to identify.

The concept of a world that is a machine or a clockwork implied the existence of a divine craftsman or a divine clockmaker. Machines after all don't put themselves together. In this way, the mechanical philosophy could be viewed as supporting religion. We'll have a lot more to say about this position and its developments down to the present day in our next lecture. For now, I will only point out that, already in the 17th century, some thinkers were quick to realize that the kind of god this argument suggested was not necessarily orthodox. For example, it could suggest an absentee god—in other words, a god that built the clock, set it in motion, and then took a vacation; he went away. How would this conception fit with the Catholic doctrine of the continuation of miracles or with the more generally Christian notion of a providential and personal god?

But this was only one problem with the mechanical philosophy. The mechanical philosophy also ran to the risk of promoting materialism, that is, the belief that matter is all there is. No spiritual, no immaterial entities like the soul or God. If matter and motion was so powerful as an explanatory tool, can't it just explain everything? It's not hard to see that materialism eviscerates theistic belief because it renders nonexistent the central objects of religion: God and the human soul.

Materialism, bad enough on its own, further invoked the danger of determinism; that is, the belief that all future events are unavoidably determined by current conditions. As it has sometimes been expressed—at least before the advent of modern physics—if we knew the position and the motion of every atom in the universe, then we could predict all future positions and, thus, all future events. So in a materialistic world without entities that are both external to matter and able to interact with it, then all the motions of particles on their own determine everything—all future events; in other words, no free will.

Gassendi was very aware of these possible outcomes, hence he was careful to posit the immaterial soul for man. But a contrary voice was the mathematician and political theorist, Thomas Hobbes. He embraced a mechanical philosophy in his own way and took it so far as to propose a corporeal god as a corporeal human soul. His contemporaries read this as equivalent to atheism. Whether or not Hobbes was truly an atheist, in our sense of the term, remains a subject of debate. But 17th-century readers read him as one; his views threw the danger of the overextension of mechanism into high relief.

Let me pause now to make an important observation. In the modern world, we are likely to know a significant number of people who are atheists, either avowedly so or practically so. Thus, it's easy for us to forget how extraordinarily outlandish such a position would have seemed in the 17th century. Sure, some people went about their lives ignoring the existence of God, but that's easy to dismiss as just ignorance or immorality. But actual considered philosophical atheism was essentially unheard of. Nonetheless, the 17th century, particularly in England, marked a time when people began worrying seriously about the rise of atheism. By the late 17th century, atheists were thought to be hiding behind every bush, like terrorists today. But in fact, it proved essentially impossible to point to a specific person and say, "There's an atheist." Not that that did anything to allay the concern, the worry was that they were out there somewhere.

Let me stress, not only was this concern a new one in the 17th century, but also that it has continued to characterize religious, particularly Protestant, apologetics ever since. Don't underestimate this change. Medieval religious writers spent their time arguing for subtle understandings of the Trinity or of free will or of divine providence or of the Eucharist. In the 17th century began a shift in religious writings towards apologetics and frankly to the trivial, to arguing simply for the existence of some kind of deity. The emergence of this concern over atheism therefore had a profound impact on both science and theology.

Now to return to the mechanical philosophy. Numerous responses to the mechanical philosophy were proposed in order to address its potential overextension to materialism, atheism, and other theologically unacceptable positions. One response came from a group of thinkers called the Cambridge Platonists. They were a group of professors at Cambridge University in the second half of the 17th century who took particular inspiration from Platonic and Neo-Platonic ideas. One of them, by the name of Henry More, argued that brute matter and motion were simply insufficient to produce the world we see and the natural phenomena we see. So he added to matter and motion an inherent guiding principle. This guiding principle was a non-sentient, but immaterial entity he called the "spirit of nature" or the "plastic principle." This principle could explain the remarkable organization of matter. The way, for example, that a seed could draw in water and nutrients and generate therefrom perfectly intricately formed leaves and flowers. It guided the shaping of complex organisms, hence the name, "plastic principle." That doesn't mean it's cheap and made in China; what it means is that it comes from the Greek word *plastikos*, meaning a person who molds images from clay.

Some thinkers didn't think much of this idea. One contemporary who rejected it was Robert Boyle. Boyle objected that the plastic principle was an unnecessary intermediary between God and creation. God was smart enough, he said, to have created a world to run on its own perfectly well without having this host of maintenance workers running around keeping it going. But, at the same time, Boyle explicitly wished Henry More the best of luck in trying to prove the existence of some kind of immaterial entity; spirit of nature just wasn't the right one. We will see in a minute that Boyle himself was on the hunt for spiritual entities as well.

Robert Boyle will be familiar to any of you on account of the gas law that's named after him, Boyle's Law, namely that the pressure and volume of the gas are inversely proportional. But Boyle did much, much more. In fact, so involved was Boyle specifically in natural philosophy and religion and their interactions that we should spend some time specifically with him. Boyle is an old friend of mine, so let me make some introductions.

Boyle was born into the richest family in Britain in 1627. After a brief and not terribly successful attempt to write moral and devotional treatises, he turned his attention to natural philosophy, especially chemistry. Having a steady income from inheritance and remaining unmarried, Boyle spent his life experimenting and writing. His over 50 books contained important scientific essays, subtle philosophical analyses, and theological treatises.

Boyle was a deeply religious man, Anglican in profession, though fairly ecumenical in his thought. He viewed the role of the natural philosopher—what we would call today a scientist—as a priest of nature; that's his term. What does he mean by that? He saw the study of the natural world as an inherently religious activity. The role of the natural philosopher was to study the world and to gather up from the world ways in which to praise the creator. Like the priest sacrificing in the temple, the scientist in the world is the conduit for the silent hymns and prayers of the natural world to God.

The idea that the study of the natural world was religious and devotional was not an uncommon perspective in the 17th century. It's linked, of course, to the doctrine of the Two Books, the Book of Scripture and the Book of Nature, that we discussed before. Reading the Book of Nature, that is, studying the natural world, was learning about God, very simply. Indeed, Boyle suggested in fact that scientific activity—natural philosophical activity—was a particularly appropriate thing to do on Sundays. Why? Because it was a kind of worship. In fact, one of Boyle's earliest essays was entitled *The Book of Nature*, and it dealt exactly with the issue of how natural studies strengthened and inspired religious devotion. At the other end of his life, Boyle's last book was entitled *The Christian Virtuoso* and here the word "virtuoso" means about the same as natural philosopher. It was written to explain Boyle's own life, and as well as an invitation to join him in his project. It dismisses the idea, which apparently must have begun to arise at this period, that scientific study might somehow be deleterious to religious life and belief. Boyle will have none of it. He makes the opposite case—scientific study and understanding leads us to a profounder and more just appreciation of Christianity and a greater devotion to God.

Now remember, that in the late 17th century, there was a certain atheism panic. Boyle was one of the worried parties. This search was particularly crucial in England—the search for a solution to the atheism panic, that is—thanks to the new Anglican doctrine of the cessation of miracles, as I mentioned earlier. Without the possibility of miraculous events that could signal the special activity of God in the world, Anglicans had to look for other events that could signal the existence and activity of supernatural beings. Thus there were many projects at this time to uncover evidences of spiritual activity in the world, particularly of spiritual entities like demons, angels, ghosts, and so forth. Boyle himself was involved in several of these projects. Boyle's name, in fact, appeared for the first time in print in connection with his sponsorship of a translation of a French book entitled *The Devil of Mascon.*

This book provides the account of a poltergeist that haunted a minister in France. Boyle also helped out a contemporary of his by the name of Joseph Glanvill, who was collecting witchcraft testimony. Boyle himself was interested in witches, not because they are evil, but because their activities, if they could be verified, could demonstrate spiritual forces. Boyle recognized perfectly well that the vast majority of such accounts were bogus. But he also realized that he needed to find only one or a few creditable accounts to argue his case that there was spirit activity in the world. Boyle also collected what he called "strange" reports, uncanny, possibly supernatural occurrences that could argue for spiritual activity. He actually planned to publish this collection later in life, but apparently thought better of it, and so it exists only in manuscript.

Boyle also spoke to some who attempted to practice the Dark Arts. In one book, he tells of "inquisitive men," as he calls them, who have so desired to prove the existence of spiritual substances that they have tried, "forbidden ways of attaining satisfaction and many have chosen rather to venture the putting themselves within the power of demons than remain ignorant whether or not there are any such beings." "As I have learned," he says, "by the private acknowledgments made to me of such unhappy, though not unsuccessful, attempts by diverse learned men who themselves made these attempts in various places."

Boyle thought about invoking spirits himself, but its possible immorality stopped him from doing so. There's another interesting case here—Boyle was keenly interested in preparing the philosophers' stone. What is the philosophers' stone? The philosophers' stone is a material substance to be prepared in the laboratory. It was the goal of alchemists who claimed that it had the power to transform base metals like lead into gold. For now, I am not going to talk very much about alchemy, I will just say that it was a serious and a legitimate endeavor in the 17th century, undergirded by what seemed at the time quite solid and testable theories.

At any rate, Boyle came to believe that the philosophers' stone could do more than just make gold. What he came to is a very unusual belief, and we don't know exactly where this idea came from, but he claimed that the philosophers' stone might well be able to attract angels and facilitate communication with them. For the already rich Boyle, this possibility gave much more incentive to make or obtain the stone than just to use it to make gold. Indeed, he writes in an unpublished manuscript how this would prove a powerful weapon against those atheists out there, for they could be shown the existence of angels.

All of this might sound a bit odd to you, but it would be a huge mistake to dismiss it as weirdness or crankiness, regardless of your personal opinion about demons and angels. I am presenting all this material to you to show you how wide a domain early modern natural philosophers felt was theirs to investigate. Studies of spiritual phenomena were carried out by some of the most prominent natural philosophers of the day, people whose works we still rely upon for fundamental parts of modern science. To them, such studies could be as much of their investigations as chemistry or physics. Contrast this with the situation that the modern scientist has; imagine a grant proposal today to investigate angelic apparitions. How, why, and when did this shrinkage of domain occur? Let's keep this development in mind as the course progresses.

Now I have another point to make. An important characteristic of the science-religion landscape of the 17th century was the sure conviction that scientific discoveries would prove the best support for religious belief. One instance of this conviction comes from one of Boyle's last acts. In his will, he endowed a series of lectures against atheism. The first Boyle lecturer was Richard Bentley, a classical scholar, critic, philologer, and theologian. In eight lectures he delivered in 1692 and 1693, he used recent scientific discoveries to argue against atheism and in favor of a beneficent creator.

Interestingly, much of Bentley's material came from none other than Sir Isaac Newton himself. Indeed, the correspondence between Bentley and Newton still exists. Newton proposed several arguments for the existence of God from his own scientific investigations. In fact,

Bentley's lectures served in turn to help popularize some of Newton's ideas. Again we see here cooperation between science and theology.

Newton himself was deeply religious, as was the case we must remember for essentially all the scientific greats of the early modern period. Galileo and Descartes were good practicing Catholics. Gassendi and Mersenne were priests. Boyle was called a lay priest by his confessor; Boyle was so religious, it's said that he never spoke the word God without pausing before saying it. Newton was just as religious as they, except that he was a heretic. He denied, for example, the doctrine of the Trinity, and he spent time trying to identify and correct what he called "corruptions of scripture." He likewise was interested in prophecy and eschatology, that is, the study of the end of the world. By the way, Newton suggested that the world will come to an end in 2060.

His *Principia mathematica* of 1687 stands as one of the foundational texts of physics. In it, he proves the laws of falling bodies and of planetary motions and derives them all from his overarching theory of universal gravitational attraction. But in the same text, he also freely discusses the attributes and activities of God. Again, we return to the changing domain considered appropriate for scientific discussion. It was not unusual for physics texts of the time to deal with topics we would today consider religious and, therefore, inappropriate for inclusion.

Newton talked about God in the *Principia*. Gassendi discussed the soul and the general resurrection in his treatment of physics. Descartes used the immutability of God as the guarantee for his ideas about the conservation of motion. By comparing this 17th-century situation with the modern day, we once again have clear evidence for the fluid and culturally contingent boundaries between science and religion or science and theology over time.

Like many English contemporaries, Newton wanted to find evidence of divine activity in the world. Even though he was a heretic, he was very far from being an atheist. There is some evidence that he may have believed that the force of gravity he discovered and described was just such divine activity. If this were true, then it would solve a real dilemma for non-Catholic Christians. How do we get proof that God continues to care for his creation without miracles? The force of gravity is inexplicable in a billiard ball universe. Thus, it seems to lie outside the mechanical properties of matter. Newton strove to find a natural cause without ever being satisfied.

Second of all, gravity is constant. You can drop a ball at any time, and it always seems to work. As such, it is a continual witness to the action of God, but better. Being constant, it is also a fundamental part of what? The *cursus communis naturae*, the common course of nature. Indeed, only the suspension of the law of gravity would be miraculous. Thus, God can have visible activity in the world, causing gravity, without a miracle, simply by being the direct cause of a law of nature. You should realize also that such a view would, of course, move our conception of the world a little way towards supernaturalism.

Before I end this lecture, let's get back to our Boyle lecturer, Dr. Bentley. Drawing upon Newton, Bentley used the structure of the solar system as evidence of God and his design, and its stability as evidence of his providence and continued activity. For example, he says, all the planets revolve and rotate in the same direction. How could this be an effect of mere chance? The solar system remains stable. The sun has not burned out, nor have the planetary orbits deteriorated. This latter point was a real issue, for by this point in time, planetary observations were keen enough to discover that the motions of Jupiter and Saturn were not stable. One was slowing down; the other was speeding up. The system could not have survived intact all these years without some adjustment by divine intervention.

But such arguments for the existence of God are inherently problematic. Why? Because they are an appeal to ignorance, specifically our ignorance of hidden causation. Look, there's that problem again. What such arguments create is a "God of the gaps." What does that mean? The phrase "God of the gaps" refers to an image of the deity that is inadvertently created by arguments that invoke his direct intervention to explain otherwise inexplicable phenomena or situations, in other words, to close the gaps in otherwise naturalistic explanations. The problem is that such gaps tend to be manifestations of the incompleteness of our knowledge at any given time. Thus they tend to close up with the advance of scientific knowledge, thus putting religion in the embarrassing position of constant retreat. The problem, for example, of the seemingly unstable motion of Jupiter and Saturn was solved in the late 18th century using Newtonian physics, not the hand of God.

If we invest in a God of the gaps, that god risks being progressively squeezed out of the picture. The problem with the God of the gaps is a background to the belief expressed by White, Draper, and others that religion always retreats before science. But such a retreat is a historically contingent event. It depends upon a prior choice—to create and then to rely upon God of the gaps arguments.

We cannot deny that some gaps might not be able to be closed. One that comes to mind is that moment of creation when there's something out of nothing. This seems to be something that science, at least as we know it, can't address. But historically speaking, such examples are very few indeed in comparison to the many that have been proposed and filled since the 17th century.

But now we're getting a little ahead of ourselves. The use of the knowledge of the natural world to support religious belief developed extensively in the 18th and 19th century. The field became known as natural theology. Natural theology and its attendant argument from design is what we will talk about in the next lecture.

Lecture Eight
Natural Theology and Arguments from Design

Scope:

The world is full of wondrous things that evoke our admiration. Some authors, accordingly, have used the natural world to argue for the existence of the deity. Indeed, for centuries, the study of the natural world was seen as, in part, a devotional act. This lecture examines the emergence and content of *natural theology*, especially in England in the 18th and 19th centuries, and the important shift it witnesses from a personally devotional aspect of science into an expressly apologetic one. Recently, *intelligent design* (ID) has appeared as a further step in the track of natural theology. This lecture looks at historical features of both approaches and their limitations.

Outline

I. The drawing of inferences and proofs about the deity from the natural world is known as *natural theology*.

   A. Although limited theological readings of the "book of nature" have been carried out since antiquity, a developed natural theology arose only in the 17th and 18th centuries.

      1. Natural theology proved highly influential, diverse, and resilient down to the 19th century; it was especially prominent in the anglophonic world.

      2. *The Wisdom of God Manifested in the Works of Creation* (1691) by John Ray (1628–1705) is a foundational text in the genre.

      3. Many early Boyle Lectures featured natural theology, for example, Richard Bentley's 1692 sermons and the 1711 and 1712 lectures of William Durham (on physico-theology).

      4. Perhaps the most cited example is that of William Paley (1743–1805), whose 1802 *Natural Theology, or Evidences of the Existence and Attributes of the Deity Collected from the Appearances of Nature* proved enormously popular.

B. Both natural philosophers ("scientists") and clergymen wrote works on natural theology; indeed, natural theology was a meeting ground of science and religion. The *Bridgewater Treatises* (1830s) were a comprehensive collection of natural theology gleaned from various sciences and mathematics, written by some of England's leading scientific thinkers, and funded by the 8th Earl of Bridgewater.

C. Much early natural theology sprang from 17th-century mechanical conceptions of the world—a watch implies a watchmaker.

D. Although some, including Paley, argued that attributes of God (mercy, unity, providence, and so on) could be drawn from nature, the brunt of natural theology was to prove simply God's existence.

    1. Thus, the argument from design was central to natural theology.

    2. The argument from design holds that the smooth functioning and intricate contrivance of the universe implies a designer, that is, provides proof for the existence of God.

II. The argument from design was prone to criticism; upon analysis, it turned out to be weak, ambiguous, and—from the point of view of orthodox Christianity—dangerous.

  A. Natural theological arguments can result in many different kinds of a God.

    1. A watch may imply a master watchmaker, but it can also imply a company of watchmakers (that is, polytheism) or an apprentice watchmaker (a demiurge).

    2. The God of natural theology (like the "God of the philosophers") is far from the Christian God—without moral force, unique eternity, personal concern, or other attributes.

    3. Indeed, deists latched onto natural theology as much as Anglican vicars.

    4. Analogical reasoning is valid only if the analogical basis is sound—the basis on which the design argument rests is that God is like a human being. This is a dangerous anthropomorphism.

B. Pressed too forcefully, such arguments actually encourage non-Christian views of God by overemphasizing rational arguments for his mere *existence* at the expense of faith in the revelations of his *attributes*.

C. The probatory power of the argument from design is very weak.

   1. We cannot tell whether perceived design is real or an illusion; there is no possibility of comparing a designed versus an undesigned universe. There is no valid yardstick with which to measure degrees of design.

   2. The argument often relies on an appeal to ignorance; we "cannot imagine" how an intricate system could come to be without an intelligent designer.

   3. Thus, the argument from design can appeal only to *emotion* (feelings of awe and wonder), rather than to *reason*.

   4. Although possibly exhortatory in a devotional context, the design argument is unsatisfactory in a rigorously probatory (for example, scientific) one.

D. The last point highlights a crucial historical development within natural theology—namely, a shift in focus from awe at the natural world in heightening devotion in believers to its use as an apologetic to convince nonbelievers.

   1. Design is in the eye of the beholder.

   2. The propagation and popularity of the design argument stems from historical, political, social, and geographical circumstances of 18th-century England.

   3. Thus, the development of and reliance on such arguments makes sense only in a cultural context in which there is paranoia about atheism.

E. The ubiquity of natural theology and its argument from design is the necessary background to Darwin and his reception.

III. A recent redevelopment of the argument from design has appeared in the United States: *intelligent design* (ID).

A. ID holds two basic tenets:

   1. Intelligent causes have a crucial role in the origin and design of the universe and of life and its diversity.

   2. Design is empirically detectable in nature.

B. Many (but not all) supporters present ID as scientific, yet critics identify it as a thinly veiled offensive by evangelical/fundamentalist Christians to insert particular belief systems into scientific and educational establishments.

  1. The fact that ID is argued for primarily in the courts of law and public opinion (rather than in appropriate scientific organs) would seem to support this contention.

  2. For the most vocal supporters, there is a clear political and social agenda.

  3. The existence of such agendas is not necessarily damning, because historically, some scientific positions have similarly embraced political or social agendas. But it *is* a crucial part of the context.

C. Insofar as ID is akin to natural theology (that is, deploying the argument from design), it is susceptible to all the critiques, weaknesses, and problems of natural theology.

D. Some ID proponents differentiate their position from natural theology by claiming that ID is not about proving the *existence* of a designer but, rather, exploring what the *assumption* of a designer can explain.

  1. In this formulation, however, it is hard to imagine what explanatory improvements could be forthcoming.

  2. ID begins with features of the world that are, in the words of one ID proponent, "inherently inexplicable in terms of natural causes."

  3. The claim of "inherent inexplicability" is problematic and asserts that ordinary secondary causation is inadequate; thus, primary causation—the action of a designer—must be invoked.

  4. But primary causation is, by its very nature, incomprehensible to us—like a *creatio ex nihilo*.

  5. Thus, recourse to primary causation explains nothing in the usual sense of the word *explain*.

  6. When we rule out the usual functioning of natural causes, we are left with only two options: (a) direct primary causation (for example, the creation out of nothing); (b) the First Cause acts through secondary causes in such a way that their usual action is altered, for example, when an effect is disproportionate—a miracle.

7. But all we can do with such an event is to label it as such, not explain it. (If we could explain it, it would not be a miracle.)
8. The promise, therefore, that the designer might literally *explain* something is vain.
9. Human beings can comprehend only secondary causation; recourse to primary causation is an abandonment of the search for explanation and understanding. This is how medieval theologians gravitated toward the position of naturalism.

E. Methodologically favoring naturalism is a way to preserve what is the most fundamental human aspiration—the search for understanding. This applies with equal force to both science and theology.

F. Naturalism is a favorite whipping boy for ID supporters, but they conflate two different kinds of naturalism.
   1. Methodological naturalism says only that we should appeal solely to natural causes when giving explanations of natural things.
   2. But philosophical naturalism says that the natural is all that exists.
   3. Philosophical naturalism entails atheism; methodological naturalism does not.

G. ID supporters depict the scientific community as inherently atheistic and atheism as a "non-scientifically" assumed position.
   1. Considered free from context, starting positions of theism and atheism are equally faith-based (non-rational) assumptions.
   2. But in specifically scientific studies, naturalism has been a guiding *methodological principle*, favored by natural philosophers and theologians since antiquity; such naturalism need *not* imply atheism.
   3. ID's depictions of scientists are straw-man arguments; more than 40 percent of current American scientists believe in a personal God and a larger percentage (a majority), in a transcendent being.

H. We will treat ID further in the lecture on evolution, which is a central point of concern for most ID proponents.

Essential Reading:

Brooke, *Science and Religion*, chapter 6 (pp. 192–225).

William A. Dembski, "Is Intelligent Design a Form of Natural Theology?"

Supplementary Reading:

Eugenie Scott, *Creationism vs. Evolution: An Introduction.*

Questions to Consider:

1. Given that it has no power actually to explain anything any better than simply saying that the thing is inexplicable, what could be the point behind the promotion of ID?

2. What might be the causes for the "watering down" of rational and speculative medieval theology into English natural theology of the 18th and 19th centuries?

Lecture Eight—Transcript

Natural Theology and Arguments from Design

Can the study of the natural world demonstrate the existence of God? In the last lecture, we looked at how a firm conviction at the study of the natural world was a devotional activity developed into a practice of using scientific knowledge for religious apologetics. In this lecture, we are going to look more closely at the product, natural theology, and its major tool, the argument from design.

Now natural theology is defined as the drawing of inferences and proofs regarding God from the natural world. We can see how old the general concept is by noting that natural theology results, in essence, from readings of the Book of Nature. But while limited theological readings of the Book of Nature have been around since antiquity, a well-defined natural theology arose only at the end of the 17th century. Natural theology, once developed, showed great resiliency and flexibility down through the 19th century, and it was particularly prominent in the English-speaking world. That's a feature that will require some explanation.

But first, let's survey some writers in the natural theology tradition. The foundational text in the genre is a work by John Ray. Now Ray was born in 1627, the same year as Boyle. He studied at Cambridge and became especially interested in plants. He proposed some early classification systems for them, and parts of his system are still in use. In 1667, he was made a fellow of the Royal Society of London, the oldest scientific society in continuous operation, and he published prodigiously.

Ray was also ordained an Anglican priest in 1660. As such, he is another example in the long line of people in Holy Orders who were also involved in the study of the natural world. I keep bringing this point up again and again because I want to make absolutely sure that I am breaking down the rather automatic modern wrong response of putting religious thinkers and scientists into different categories.

In 1691, Ray published a book entitled *The Wisdom of God Manifested in the Works of Creation*. It proved very popular. It was reprinted frequently for over 50 years. Ray's work, like that of Boyle, Newton, and other 17th-century natural philosophers, was based on the conviction that, "There is, for a free man, no occupation more worthy and delightful than to contemplate the beauteous works of nature and honor the infinite wisdom and goodness of God." Ray's book presents material gained from all kinds of recent studies in the fields of botany, anatomy, astronomy, physiology, and so forth, all of them proclaiming the wisdom and goodness of God. In other words, the investigation of the natural world enhances reverence for its creator.

Next came the Boyle lectures. We mentioned Richard Bentley's 1692-93 sermons last time, but there were many others. For example, a particularly popular series were the 1711 and 1712 lectures given by William Durham. These were collected, revised, printed, and reprinted down to the 1760s. Durham called his subject physico-theology, that is, theology from the natural world. In 1802, however, there appeared what is probably the most widely read example of the genre, William Paley's *Natural Theology*. Paley was himself an Anglican vicar and a writer of textbooks, largely on moral philosophy. There wasn't much original material in Paley's volume, but it did summarize much of what had gone on in the natural theology tradition of the 18th century. The book was regularly read in university curricula, and it greatly impressed, among many others, a young Charles Darwin.

Finally, perhaps the most extensive work on natural theology appeared in the 1830s. These were the *Bridgewater Treatises*, an eight-volume set funded by a request [sic bequest] from the 8th Earl of Bridgewater. He left £8,000 to commission and print works, "On the power, wisdom, and goodness of God as manifested in the creation." Authors were chosen by a committee composed of the president of the Royal Society, the Bishop of London, and the Archbishop of Canterbury. The series contained works on astronomy, anatomy, chemistry, geology, and other fields.

The hundreds of works on natural theology that appeared over the course of nearly two centuries were written by a wide variety of authors. So were they predominantly natural philosophers or clergymen? Well, often both. John Ray, as an example, his activities were evenly divided between natural philosophy and divinity, and he held credentials in both. Other authors were active predominantly in only one of the fields. Durham and Paley were clergymen without personal activity in natural philosophy. They borrowed from the works of others for their natural theological writings.

On the other side was, for an example, Bernard Nieuwentijt. He was a Dutch mathematician and a doctor of medicine. And in the 1710s, he wrote one of the few notable non-British works on natural theology. But in fact, the book went through many more printings in England than it did anywhere else. What was the main thrust of all this authorial activity? While some argued that the attributes of God could be drawn from the natural world, most natural theology was content to prove merely God's existence. This goal was already clear in John Ray. He writes:

> There is no greater, at least no more palpable and convincing argument of the existence of a deity than the admirable art and wisdom that discovers itself in the make and constitution, the order and disposition, the ends and uses of all the parts and members of the stately fabric of heaven and earth. For if, in the works of art, as for example a curious edifice or machine, counsel, design, and direction to an end appearing in the whole frame and in all the several pieces of it do necessarily infer the being in operation of some intelligent architect or engineer.

You'll see there was a shortage of periods in the late 17th century. They didn't like to use them up unnecessarily.

There is a fine example here of how most natural theology rests upon one principle: the argument from design. The argument from design holds that the smooth functioning and intricate contrivance of natural objects implies a designer. That is, it provides proof for the existence of God. Atheism was the natural theologian's prime target and signs of design, their chief weapon.

The classic example is the story of the watch. It was told by Paley in 1802, even though he collected it out of Nieuwentijt, and Nieuwentijt himself drew upon ideas connected with the mechanical philosophy. The story goes like this: Imagine one day you are out walking in an isolated place, and you see a watch lying on the ground. You pick it up, and you look at it. You open the back. You notice how beautifully the gears are cut and how perfectly they fit together. You see that the best possible materials are used to make the component parts. And you wonder where did the watch come from? From the watch, therefore, you naturally infer a watchmaker, even if there's nobody in sight and you can find no direct sign of the watchmaker, you know he must be out there somewhere, simply because you have the watch he made in your hand. The argument then moves from artificial to natural objects. Consider the eye. See how beautifully it's put together, how ingenious the adaptation of parts; therefore, looking at the eye, you are sure of the existence of a designer of the eye, which we conclude to be God.

What did people in the 18th century actually make of the argument from design? The argument from design was subject to criticism already by the middle of the 18th century and not just, or even predominantly as it turns out, from those inclined towards atheism. The argument on examination turns out to be weak, ambiguous, and from the position of orthodox Christianity, potentially dangerous.

Several thinkers, David Hume among them, pointed out that the arguments from design might not take you where you want to go. A watch might imply a master watchmaker, but it could just as easily imply a company of watchmakers, in other words, polytheism. Or it could point to an apprentice watchmaker, something akin to Plato's Demiurge, and even if we get to monotheism, the god of natural theology is far from the Christian God without moral force, unique eternity, or personal concern about the creation.

In fact, deists—in other words those who believe in a god but one who is impersonal and detached—latched on to natural theology every bit as much as Anglican vicars. Deists used it to show that Christian revelation was unnecessary. The principles of religion could be gathered entirely from nature by reason. So faith, revelation, and church are all unnecessary. When pressed too forcefully, the argument from design actually encourages non-Christian views of God. It does so by overemphasizing arguments drawn from reason for his mere existence, at the expense of faith in revelations of his attributes. You see the difference. From a Christian perspective, merely demonstrating the existence of God is really a pretty cheap commodity. So there's a designer God, big deal. He could be the God of the Neoplatonist who isn't even aware that he created the universe and who doesn't, can't even, care about you and your problems. This is totally antithetical to Christian theology that the best metaphor for God is "Father."

Besides the endpoint to the argument, there are problems with the mechanism. The argument is held together by analogy, and analogical reasoning is only as valid as the analogical basis is sound. What does that mean? Let's consider the propositions. A watch implies an intelligent watchmaker. Okay, no problem, we've seen watches being made. The proposition is then used analogically to say that the eye implies an intelligent eye maker. But this assumes that natural things, eyes, are produced like artificial things, watches. The analogy is a legacy of the mechanical philosophy, but it's questionable. Natural things arise spontaneously as units, from seeds, eggs, and such like, and they reproduce others like themselves. Artificial things, on the other hand, are composites assembled piece by piece. And I, at home, have a drawer full of watches, but I've never opened the drawer to find they've given birth to new ones.

A second assumption is that God, the maker of natural things, works like a human being, the maker of artificial things. Well, besides being inherently unlikely, this is dangerous as anthropomorphism. It brings God down to a human level. It threatens to make his activity banal, mechanical to be precise, and rob him of transcendence.

Worse still is that design is often in the eye of the beholder. We cannot tell whether what we perceive as design is real or our construct. We cannot put a designed universe next to an undesigned one and compare the difference. There's no valid control, no valid yardstick by which to measure degrees of design. Another way of saying this is to point out that the argument *from* design depends first upon an argument *for* design. That is, we must first demonstrate clearly that there is transcendent design, and that will be impossible unless we can compare how things turn out with design to how they turn out without design.

Arguments *for* design in the world rely ultimately upon appeals to ignorance. We, say, cannot imagine how an intricate system could come to be without an intelligent designer. All such arguments lead, as we've seen, to a god of the gaps. We don't currently have a way to explain what we see, and so we resort to God as an explanation. The arguments from and for design are not really rational arguments. What do they appeal to? They appeal to our emotions, our feelings of awe and wonder, rather than to our reason.

The world is an extraordinary place. It is full of marvels, but you can't turn admiration into an argument. Therefore, while design arguments are great for exhortation in a devotional context, they are unsatisfactory in a probatory one. This point now highlights a crucial historical development, a shift in what natural theology was actually asked to do. Initially, natural theology was about heightening devotion in believers. It was thus intensely personal. But this function was progressively displaced in favor of a public use as an apologetic to convince nonbelievers. That's where the weakness lies. While reading the Book of Nature can fulfill the first goal, it's not able to accomplish the second. It's easier to augment a fire than to start one.

A believer studying the marvelous intricacies of the natural world can see the hand of God and have his devotion increased, but a nonbeliever, while subject to the very same feelings of awe and wonder, is not going to translate that emotional response into praise of a creator. Instead, he could just as easily marvel at the efficiency and power of the operation of natural causes. In short, a sense of wonder is going to enhance your respect for whatever cause you already have in mind, not change its identity.

We shouldn't overlook the hand of history. Natural theology's development stems largely from circumstances particular to 18th-century England. First, the reliance on such arguments makes sense only in a context where there's already paranoia about atheism. Second, there was, specifically in England, pressure to turn to reason for religious apologetic because of the political situation. The English Civil War of the mid-17th century left a legacy of religious dissension and sectarianism, especially by "low" church enthusiasts as they are called, namely, people who relied on personal experiences of faith or revelation and who opposed the Church of England. One solution was to turn to reasoned-based arguments instead of faith- or Bible-based ones, with the assumption that reason is something everybody can agree on.

The members of the Royal Society believed that experimental natural philosophy was also something that people of differing religious commitments could agree on. Thus, with the social and political need to restore order and unity in Britain, the alliance of natural philosophy and religious apologetic was a natural solution.

Thirdly, there's something very English about the image of a proper, well-ordered world governed by a beneficent sovereign. Indeed, the similarity between the natural theologian's view of the world and the projected image of the English state and crown has been remarked upon by many historians. There is also a social specificity. You are far more likely to come up with or buy into the idea that the world is perfectly designed by a benevolent deity if you are a country vicar sipping sherry, looking out into your garden; more so than if you are a peasant in a hovel trying to scrape a few beans out of a lousy plot of land and half of your children die before the age of 10. In the same way, England's green and pleasant land suggests an agreeable natural theology better than would a harsher environment like Central Africa.

Now let's bring the discussion up to the present. A development related to natural theology has recently appeared in the United States. It's called intelligent design or, since everything scientific has to have an acronym, ID. Let's have a look at it. There are two general principles to intelligent design. The first is that intelligent causes have a crucial role in the origin and design of the universe and of life in its diversity. The second is that design is empirically detectable in nature. Well, some ID advocates deny that their intelligent cause is God. But this is a lost cause. ID must terminate in a divinity of some sort. Let me explain.

For example, some ID proponents would allow that hyper-intelligent space aliens could be the designer. But this is no ultimate answer, for then one would have to ask who designed the hyper-intelligent space aliens? The only escape from an infinite regress, as Aristotle and St. Thomas would explain patiently, is an undesigned designer, prior to all designed things and therefore the first designer or first cause. And once you have an intelligent first cause, you have a divinity by definition, not the Christian God to be sure, but God nonetheless.

Some critics would find the recognition that ID, regardless of its disclaimers, must be theistic as damning criticism. I don't think this is the case at all. It needn't be. A theistic commitment didn't undermine the important scientific work in contributions of Kepler, Galileo, Boyle, Newton, and you can name any number of them. But some critics have identified ID as a thinly veiled, perhaps disingenuous, move by evangelical fundamentalist Christians to insert what they can of their particular belief systems into scientific and educational establishments.

Well this accusation gained some support from the fact that ID proponents have often adopted legal or political strategies or appealed to the court of public opinion to compel assent to their claims. If ID is a scientific theory, as its proponents claim, then it has to be assessed by scientists, by the slow, very difficult route of accumulating argument, evidence, result, and supporters. I know of lots of examples in the history of science where claims initially and long-rejected by the majority of natural philosophers were eventually shown to be true.

They became the accepted view. But I'm unaware of a precedent or a philosophical justification for having a scientific point determined by a law court or public opinion. The scientific lies beyond the competency of both. So therefore, legal maneuvering looks like an end run around scientific discourse. And since actions tend to speak louder than words, it does tend to undercut ID's claims to be scientific.

Further, it's been pointed out that vocal supporters of ID have clear, generally highly conservative, sociopolitical agenda. Again, some critics consider this damning evidence, but as a historian of science, I'm afraid again I have to disagree. The existence of such agendas is not necessarily damning. Some scientific positions of the past have also embraced political and social agendas, or even emerged out of them. Origins and agendas are crucial parts of the context, but they're not sufficient ground for dismissing claims.

So what's the promise of intelligent design? Many people adopt intelligent design in a way that connects it to the natural theology tradition, namely, as religious apologetic. They believe there's design in nature, and this argues for a designer. But this version of ID is susceptible to all the problems, weaknesses, and dangers that natural theology was. We explored these previously. I'm not going to recap all the arguments now, just rewind the lecture and listen to them again; they all apply.

Some other ID supporters, however, strive to distance their system from natural theology.

> Instead of arguing for the existence of a designer [writes one major exponent of ID] …intelligent design asks how positing an intelligent cause to explain such objects offers fresh scientific insights. …The point is to see what a designer helps explain. The point is not to establish the existence of the designer.

Well this turns the natural theology argument around. Instead of showing design in the world and arguing thence to a creator, ID, in this formulation, assumes the designer as an explanatory tool.

Since I showed above that the ultimate designer must be divine, this version of ID begins with the adoption, provisional or otherwise, of a theistic perspective. As far as I am concerned, that's fine, as it's no more inherently likely or unlikely as a starting point than an atheistic one. But here's the rub: our author says the point is to see what a designer helps explain. Okay, that sounds pretty reasonable at first glance. Assume a designer, a provisional cause for a phenomenon, and see where it takes you. The first response is, "Great. Okay guys, carry on. Let's see the results." But on second consideration, I am still happy to say, "Carry on," but on consideration, I find it hard to imagine what explanatory improvements could possibly be forthcoming. For the same advocate asserts that:

> Intelligent design begins with features of the world that are inherently inexplicable in terms of natural causes—not merely features of the world that, for now, lack a natural cause explanation, but rather for which natural causes are, in principle, incapable of providing an explanation.

This sounds to me like an attempt to wedge open a gap in which to house a god of the gaps. How on earth do we distinguish between temporary inexplicability and permanent inexplicability without having first in hand a total and complete understanding of all natural causation? And why would we trouble ourselves to uncover more about natural causation if we begin with the assumption that whatever we find will be inadequate even before we know what it is?

Just for the sake of argument, let's imagine that one has identified something in the world that is "inherently inexplicable in terms of natural causes." If you were trying to prove the existence of God, you're done. You found something demonstrably not naturally caused. Then it must be supernaturally caused; therefore, God exists. Congratulations, go home. But remember, this author claims that the point is to see what a designer helps explain.

When we claim that something is inherently inexplicable in terms of natural causes, we are asserting that ordinary secondary causation is inadequate and, therefore, that primary causation, the action of a designer, must be invoked. But primary causation is, by its very nature, incomprehensible, like in my former example, suddenly turning a cucumber into an aardvark. So the recourse to primary causation explains nothing in the usual sense of the word "explain." Do you see where we've ended up?

When we rule out the usual functioning of natural causes, we're left with only two options: one, direct primary causation; the first cause acts without mediation, for example, the creation out of nothing. Or two, the first cause acts through secondary causes in such a way that their usual action is altered, for example, when an effect is disproportionate to the cause. What do we call such events? Miracles. But once we identify a miracle, all we can do is label it as such, not explain how it took place. If we could explain it, it wouldn't be a miracle. Therefore, the promise that the designer might literally explain something is vain. This is how, in fact, the medieval theologians gravitated towards a position of naturalism. Primary causation is literally incomprehensible. Try to imagine, to actually understand, how God created something out of nothing. You can't do it. So primary causation doesn't help you if you want explanation or understanding.

Either we study secondary causation or we have nothing left to study. We can comprehend only secondary causation; therefore, only secondary causation provides true explanation, unless we want the change the meaning of the word "explanation." Recourse to primary causation is an abandonment of the search for explanation and understanding. A designer might very well be behind the secondary causes, behind them, directing them, but we can never know for sure. And in a practical sense, it doesn't make any difference for our explanations because all we can actually ever observe is the secondary causation. Thus, methodologically favoring naturalism is a way to preserve what is the most fundamental human aspiration—the search for understanding. And this applies with equal force to both science and theology.

Interestingly enough, naturalism is a favorite whipping boy for ID supporters. But they conflate two flavors of naturalism. Naturalism as a methodological principle says only that we should appeal only to natural causes for our explanations. Philosophical naturalism, on the other hand, says that the natural is all there is. Philosophical naturalism entails atheism. Methodological naturalism does not. Confusing the two leads to a depiction of the scientific establishment as inherently atheistic and atheism as a non-scientifically assumed position. Well this last part, the ID supporters have right; atheism could never be a scientifically held position. But it misses the point. The notion that favoring naturalism for explanations entails atheism is just false. Explanations based on naturalism have been favored since antiquity by natural philosophers and orthodox theologians alike. Atheism obviously was not an unavoidable part of the package then, and it isn't now.

The depiction of the scientific community as atheistic is part of a straw man argument. Recent surveys show that more than 40 percent of active American scientists believe in a personal God and a larger percentage, in fact the majority, in some kind of transcendent being; in fact, a transcendent being closer to the Judao-Islamo-Christian God, then ID's vague intelligent causes. Yet the vast majority of these scientists rely implicitly or explicitly on methodological naturalism in their daily work without being atheists.

The point is, as I've said above, if you want explanations, you have to appeal to secondary causation. The appeal to primary causation simply ends the inquiry by providing an answer without an explanation. We will revisit intelligent design briefly in lecture eleven. In the next lecture, we are going to ask questions about the age and origin of the earth and the universe.

Lecture Nine
Geology, Cosmology, and Biblical Chronology

Scope:

How old is the Earth and the universe? One can count backwards through the biblical begats to get a figure, but late-18th-century geology began to reveal a vastly older Earth. This lecture looks at attempts to date the Earth, the hints that it is vastly older than the Bible implies, and the responses from religious figures to this redating. Similarly, cosmogonic (origin of the universe) speculation has involved both scientific and theological minds equally over time. Significantly, the historical "battle lines" between rival interpretations of both the Earth's and the universe's ages and origins do not map out on simple religion/science lines but, instead, reveal a more complex picture rooted largely in social and professional differences.

Outline

I. The ages and origins of the Earth and the universe are important topics for both science and religion.

    A. In the Middle Ages, there was little reason to think that the Earth and universe were older than a few thousand years.

        1. The Bible was one of the oldest texts known, and there was no alternative evidence to contradict (or significantly supplement) its Old Testament chronology.

        2. In a homocentric universe, there would be no point to an Earth much older than man.

    B. Renaissance humanists, such as J. J. Scaliger, compiled chronologies using both biblical and other written sources.

II. In the 17th century, new scientific theories were grafted onto these earlier narratives.

    A. Fossils and geological strata gained attention and importance in the 17th century, although their meaning was ambiguous.

        1. Nicholas Steno (a Danish convert to Catholicism and now a *beatus*) studied strata and fossils in Tuscany and developed geological theories for their formation.

2. He argued four important points: (a) Fossils are the remains of living creatures; (b) rock strata are sedimentary deposits; (c) because the strata are sediments, they must have been laid down horizontally; thus, wherever we see them at an angle, they must have been shifted at some time subsequent to their formation; and (d) the lower strata must be older than the higher strata.

3. Steno was one of the first to view the surface of the Earth as a historical record.

B. At the end of the 17th century, there were attempts to intertwine biblical and geological histories into theories of the Earth.

1. One of these attempts was Thomas Burnet's *Sacred Theory of the Earth*, in which he posited six geological ages that were punctuated by cataclysmic biblical events. An example is his claim that the world, as originally formed, had a smooth surface, but at some point, it cracked and collapsed, releasing subterranean waters recorded in Scripture as Noah's Flood.

2. In 1694, the astronomer Edmund Halley critiqued Burnet's theory. Halley suggested that collision with a comet knocked the Earth's axis off vertical, causing geological devastation and Noah's Flood.

3. In 1695, John Woodward argued that the specificity of fossils to particular strata was the result of settling out from Noah's Flood.

C. The Flood thus became a *geological* event, not just a biblico-historical event, and was tied in to natural theology.

III. New naturalistic theories for origins of the Earth were proposed in the 18th century by Buffon and Laplace.

A. These progressively increased the age of the Earth, particularly the pre-human period.

B. Curiously, such theories were used simultaneously both for and against the reliability of biblical narratives. Such perspectives had social and political backgrounds and implications.

1. The contemporaneous development of "higher criticism"—begun with J. G. Eichhorn's *Die Urgeschichte* (1779), which stressed the historical contextualization of Genesis and uncovered its multiple authorship—played into this discussion.
2. Some used the findings to reject Genesis entirely, but others saw it as liberating the Bible's spiritual content by emphasizing its meager value for accurate history and chronology.

IV. In the 19th century, two related splits appeared (particularly in Britain): between philosophical geologists and Mosaical geologists and between "high" and "low" biblical interpreters.

A. The early 19th century saw the professionalization of geology—these professionals are known as the *philosophical geologists.*

B. Their opponents were the *Mosaical geologists*, who endeavored to conform scientific findings to literal readings of Genesis.

C. Significantly, there were clerics and believers in *both* groups; this fact disallows a simple science-versus-religion reading. Importantly, the division among churchmen broke down in large part along the lines of biblical criticism—between "higher" and "lower" criticism.

D. The divisions within geology and theology, then, reveal a social split between elite and popular.
1. Methodological naturalism functioned to define professional geologists.
2. The popular views stemmed in large part from an alienation from increasingly complex, esoteric, and professionalized scientific *and* theological communities.
3. This cultural reaction would recur and would (in the United States) factor strongly in the rise of fundamentalism.
4. Thus, social and intellectual distinctions proved to be of greater importance than religious distinctions in this scientific controversy.
5. Mosaicist treatments found currency for much of the 19th century in popularizing texts.

V. Questions about the age and origin of the universe are closely related to these issues.

    A. One of the earliest and most significant impacts of reason on faith involved speculation about creation.

        1. The Christian doctrine of *creatio ex nihilo* stemmed from rational arguments.

        2. Many theologians in the patristic and medieval periods wrote and speculated extensively about the creation (for example, its speed and form). They produced an entire genre of writings on this topic (hexameral treatises); these stressed naturalism.

        3. Spans of time, however, tended to remain short, in accordance with the homocentric view of creation.

        4. The notion of the eternity of the world (for example, in Aristotle) was clearly condemned.

    B. The two rival 20th-century cosmologies—steady-state and Big Bang—have had important religious impacts but not in ways clearly marking off theistic positions from atheistic ones.

        1. The Big Bang model (proposed initially in 1927 by Georges Lemaître, a Belgian priest) in its final form upholds the Christian notion of a cosmos with a definite beginning and a *creatio ex nihilo*.

        2. It was embraced by Pope Pius XII in 1951 (to the chagrin of Lemaître, who avoided theological discussion).

        3. The (now-rejected) steady-state model's loudest proponent, Fred Hoyle, frequently linked it to his atheistic and anti-clerical crusade; nonetheless, some found theological justification in it.

        4. Although it might violate the eternity criterion, it contained a continuing *creatio ex nihilo*.

VI. Progressive increases in the age of the Earth and the age and size of the universe progressively undercut the homocentric perception; thus, scientific discoveries had a direct impact on theological ideas.

Essential Reading:

Lindberg and Numbers, *God and Nature*, chapters 12–13 (pp. 296–350).

Supplementary Reading:

Brooke, *Science and Religion*, chapter 7 (pp. 226–274).

Questions to Consider:

1. The social/educational split between professional ("philosophical") geologists and Mosaicists continues in modified form to this day in the split between high-level research scientists and the general public (and, increasingly, government policymakers). How is this gap to be bridged? Can it be? Who would do it?

2. Pope Pius XII's enthusiastic reception of Big Bang cosmology and the ancient age of the universe and Earth urges the question of why some modern American fundamentalists are opposed to the concepts. Analyze the background and context of the different responses.

Lecture Nine—Transcript
Geology, Cosmology, and Biblical Chronology

Questions about the age and origin of the earth and the universe have played an important role in both scientific and theological discussions. In this lecture, we are going to look at some historical developments in both areas. This lecture will showcase two important things: first, examples of how scientific advances are or are not accommodated by adjustments in religious thought, and second, how different groups can take the same scientific finding and draw diametrically opposed theological lessons from it.

In the Patristic period and the Middle Ages, there was little reason to think that the earth was any more than a few thousand years old. Now this may sound peculiar to us because we are used to thinking of an earth that's billions of years old. But there was no reason for the Medievals, for example, to think of a concept of "deep time," as it's sometimes called. There was no physical evidence that would suggest this to them. In terms of human history, the available records did not stretch very far back. They, of course, had the writings of Greek antiquity, like Plato and Aristotle, but this pushed back human history only a few centuries before the birth of Christ.

The oldest text that the Middle Ages possessed were the early books of the Old Testament. And so these were virtually the only source for a chronology of what they would at least have considered "deep time." So toting up all the begats and the ages of the Old Testament patriarchs gave a figure for the appearance of Adam, the first man, of about 4,000 years before the birth of Christ. As for the age of the earth, even though as I've said before, there was little support for the notion that creation took place over six literal days; there was even less reason to stretch the period out into an enormous age. Given a homocentric cosmology, that is, a view of the earth and universe created for mankind, what would be the point of having an earth or universe hanging around for eons or even millennia without human beings?

With no compelling sources available, there was no reason to pass beyond the ready-to-hand figures available in the Old Testament. But I should emphasize here that these figures for the date of the earth, the age of the earth, were not held, so to speak, religiously—I mean as an article of faith or doctrine. There was just nothing around to contradict them.

Some of you will have heard of the famous date of October 23, 4004 B.C., a date given for creation. This figure resulted from the 17th-century calculations of James Ussher, the Archbishop of Armagh in Ireland. The date has sometimes been held up to ridicule, but Ussher's date, even though it is of unusual precision, was only one of many figures of about this value, give or take a few millennia, which were proposed in the early modern period. The reason we know Ussher's date in particular is that that's the one that was chosen to be put into the margin of some early editions of the King James Bible.

Nowadays, fossils and sedimentary strata provide key dating evidence for geologists. And it was in the 17th century that new attention was fixed on these features. But their meaning was ambiguous. Were fossils really the remains of living creatures? Or were they just oddly shaped rocks, that is, sports or games of nature, as they were sometimes called? One important person in this area was Niels Stensen, a Dane born in 1638 and better known by his Latinized name, Nicholas Steno. His first studies were actually in anatomy. He discovered a salivary duct that, to this day, bears his name—it's called Stensen's duct. But during his time in Italy under the patronage of the Medici, Steno collected fossils and studied rock formations. I should also say that about the same time, Steno converted to Catholicism. He became a priest and then a bishop and is now, in fact, a beatus, so one step from recognized sainthood.

Steno, in his geological work, argued four important points: first, that fossils are in fact the remains of living creatures; second, that the layers we see in rocks—what we call strata, using the Latin word for roads—are sedimentary deposits. The fossil shells found encased in these deposits were laid down with mud that later hardened into rock. Third, since the strata are sediments, they must have been laid down horizontally. Therefore, in any case where we see them at an angle, they must have been shifted at some time subsequent to their formation. Fourth and finally, it then follows that the lower strata must be older than the higher strata.

Steno couldn't determine the actual age in numbers of the strata or the fossils, but what he did do was to show that there was some development of the earth. Shells moved from the ocean now to high land; rocks formed from mud, and strata were disturbed. In other words, Steno was the first to view the surface of the earth as a historical record, a geological history, another chapter in the Book of Nature to be read.

A little while after Steno, at the end of the 17th century, there were attempts to interweave biblical and geological histories into theories of the earth. One attempt was Thomas Burnet's 1680s *Sacred Theory of the Earth*. He posited six geological ages that were punctuated by cataclysmic biblical events. For example, the world as originally formed was perfectly smooth on its surface, like an eggshell. But at some point, this shell cracked and collapsed, releasing subterranean waters, which were recorded in scripture as Noah's Flood, and leaving what Burnet calls, a wreck of a world. Here, in calling it a wreck of a world, what he is showing is typical 17th-century distaste for what were considered horrible, ugly piles of waste. We call them the Alps and other mountains.

In 1694, the astronomer Edmond Halley, of Halley's Comet fame, gave a paper to the Royal Society in which he critiqued what he called the many insufficiencies of Burnet's theory. He said, "They are as jarring as much with the physical principles of nature as with Holy Scripture." Halley suggested that collision with a comet might have knocked the earth's axis out of the vertical, making therefore the sea slosh out of its bed, causing geological devastation and the event recorded as Noah's Flood.

Just a year later, John Woodward's *An Essay Toward a Natural History of the Earth* argued that Steno's strata were in fact the result of the flood. This explained the specificity of fossils to particular strata. That is, the fossils settled out in order of density. These developments display two features of interest. First, the flood of Noah became a geological, not just a biblical, event. Second, note how new scientific findings are guiding biblical interpretation. There is little in the Genesis account of Noah to suggest geological effects of the scale envisioned by Burnet, Woodward, or their many followers.

With the discovery of physical records of geological upheavals, Genesis, as the oldest written record, might, they thought, give a parallel verbal account. Each might fill gaps in the other. What these early writers were trying to do is to piece together an earth history from all available sources, and all of them, whether physical or scriptural, were meager, incomplete, and open to multiple interpretation. While natural theologians in England were contentedly harmonizing the Bible with new natural philosophical ideas, across the channel in France, the same ideas were being used simply to discard biblical narratives. Thus it was in France that the earth's history was extended back in time to include the origins of the earth itself.

In the mid-18th century, Georges-Louis Leclerc, Comte de Buffon, hypothesized that a large comet struck the edge of the sun, knocked out from it a great plume of matter far into space. This matter then, under the action of gravity, coalesced into the planets, creating the solar system. In 1796, Pierre Simon Laplace proposed an alternative hypothesis; that the sun and planets formed simultaneously out of the condensation of a rotating nebular cloud. Nowadays, both systems of satellite formation have been shown to be correct in different ways: Laplace's nebular hypothesis for the formation of the solar system and something akin to Buffon's impact for the earth-moon system.

How Buffon and Laplace got to this point is of great interest. Remember that Newton was impressed that all planets and satellites orbit and rotate in the same direction and nearly in the same plane. This for him was evidence of design. It seemed wildly improbable that this could come about by chance. But about 50 years later, Buffon actually did the calculation. He found that the chances were 1 in about 7.7 million. But rather than suggesting the hand of God, to Buffon, it suggested that a single event had produced all the planetary motions simultaneously. He thus proposed that a comet striking a rotating sun would do just this, and Laplace had the same issues in mind. Listen carefully and you will hear a gap for the god of the gaps slamming shut.

This showcases a problem with the argument from design and some arguments from probability that still appear today. The choice between design and wildly improbable chance is generally a false dichotomy because it leaves out an essential feature: a mechanism of formation. Probability calculations have to take into account the mechanism of getting from the initial state to the final state.

For planets and satellites to come together randomly and each acquire a given motion and a given plane and in the same direction is 7.7 million to 1 against, but once we add Laplace's mechanism of formation, it drops to 1 to 1, and it becomes improbable that the solar system could be otherwise. The effect was to increase the age of the earth tremendously, specifically to create a long pre-human period.

Curiously, the new theories were used simultaneously both for and against the reliability of biblical narratives. Thus, the impact of the new science on theology was determined largely by external factors. Here is what I mean. Many French thinkers of the Enlightenment are already committed to deism over Christianity so they used the new natural evidence to ridicule the Old Testament as the superstitions of a primitive people. Voltaire, for example, ever ready to oppose established religion, even denied the specific placement of fossils in particular strata largely because this observation had been used to undergird the reality of Noah's Flood. In the 1790s, a Scottish deist, James Hutton, embraced an eternalist perspective, clearly contrary to Christian doctrine, saying that the earth shows "neither vestige of a beginning nor prospect of an end."

On the other side of the fence, Christian apologists, or just those supporting the existing socio-religious political order, harmonized new developments with scripture, and their interpretations were ever less and less naively literal. Laplace's nebula, for instance, was easily seen by some as "the world without form, and void" of Genesis I verse 2. While Laplace shocked Napoleon by claiming he did not need God as a hypothesis in the formation of the solar system, while Laplace did this, three of the *Bridgewater Treatises* worked the nebular hypothesis into natural theology.

The same theory rejected as atheistic by some for others confirmed a biblical narrative. So the same theories of evidence—and evidence could be applied in diametrically opposing ways, co-opted to fit with an individual's foregoing commitments. The same dichotomous impact greeted a contemporaneous development in biblical exegesis. What I am referring to is higher criticism. Higher criticism is the analysis of the Bible, not from a theological perspective, but from a historical, textual, and philological perspective. It thus involves issues of dating, style, and authorship.

J.G. Eichhorn's *Die Urgeschichte* (*Ancient History*), of 1779, is generally seen as the beginning of higher criticism. It uncovered, among other things, the multiple authorship of the Old Testament. Rather than being the start-to-finish composition of Moses, there are actually four authorial groups within the first five books of the Old Testament, distinguished by style and vocabulary. And this explains, for example, the discrepant accounts of creation in Genesis I and II.

Deists and others inclined to oppose Christianity on personal or political grounds claimed that higher criticism just showed the Old Testament was worthless. But many German theologians and intellectual Christians embraced higher criticism, perceiving that by emphasizing the Bible's meager value for literal chronology, it liberated its spiritual content, its spiritual message. So at the end of the 18th century, we find a complicated mess of conflicting interpretations, motivations, and agendas surrounding the question of the age of the earth. Those who just wanted to study earth history were in a sense caught in the middle. Every discovery they made could be turned by those with larger agendas into an argument for or against Christianity. The response was to band together and to professionalize.

The year 1807 saw the foundation of the Geological Society of London. The professionalization of science is possibly the most significant scientific development of the entire 19th century. These emerging professionals saw themselves as "philosophical," as they called it, geologists. Their group was defined by a focused attention to geology per se, not its religious ramifications. But of course, whenever you define one group, you define two: those inside and those outside. On the outside lived what were called the "Mosaical" geologists. They endeavored to conform scientific findings to literal readings of Genesis, and their motivation came from two sources: first, a need to oppose the rhetoric of eternalists like Hutton, and two, the moral horror at the disaster of the recent French Revolution, which many in England saw as the direct result of anti-Christian and anti-establishment tendencies exemplified by the French deists.

Also, the professionalization of geology provoked a reactionary dynamic. A field once open to all was now closing up behind intellectual, social, and educational barriers. Significantly, the same group, the Mosaical geologists, were being shut out of biblical exegesis by a higher criticism. So in the Middle Ages, for example, theologians were one of the most highly professionalized groups. Their borders were clear. But with the rise of Protestantism, there was the notion that anybody could interpret scripture. Around 1800, with the advent of higher criticism, which required high-level skills like a mastery of ancient languages, the reading of scripture was again professionalizing. Thus those with less education, less professional training, found themselves becoming excluded.

Now, if you find yourself becoming alienated, excluded from increasingly complex esoteric and professionalized scientific and theological communities, one response is retrenchment. Thus Mosaical geologists returned to late 17th-century styles of earth histories, as if the 18th century hadn't happened. Likewise, they preferred naïvely literal readings of Genesis as if higher criticism hadn't happened. Bear in mind this retrenchment in the face of being left behind by advances one can't follow. We'll come back to it.

But don't go away with the thought that the philosophical geologists were all secularists and the Mosaicists clergymen. Not at all; in fact, there were clergy on both sides of the divide, devout Christians on both sides of the divide. This fact disallows a simple science versus religion reading of the two groups; the division was really a social one, and it was enforced by how the groups treated geological knowledge publicly. This is an important point. Mosaicists directed it to apologetic purposes, akin to natural theology. The philosophical geologists frowned at this use. Even if some of their number agreed in principle with harmonizing Genesis with geology, the maintenance of their professional boundaries required that this not be done publicly.

A strict adherence to naturalism thus became a hallmark to differentiate philosophical geologists from Mosaicists, as it would become in due course for all the sciences. Remember, this stance for the philosophical geologist is not about private belief, but about what is appropriate for professional discussion and publication. Even though it can look like a science-religion split, that's not what it is. It is a social split into an elite group with training and a popular group.

It is easy, I think, to feel sympathy for the Mosaicists. We can all feel a little bit of what they felt whenever we open up a journal devoted to a topic we are sincerely interested in and discover that we need an advanced degree just to get past the first few lines. The long earth history revealed by geologists was fairly easily accommodated in the end by better educated, less literalist, biblical exegetes. For example, some developed the "day-age" theory. That assigned a vast geological epoch to each of the six days in Genesis. But there was another extension of the timeline coming in regard to the age of the universe, before the creation or the appearance of a primordial earth, depending on how you look at it.

Some of the earliest and most significant impacts of reason on faith involved speculation about creation. Particularly, the *creatio ex nihilo*, the creation out of nothing. For God's eternity to be unique, he must have created everything out of nothing—really nothing, no time, no space. In regard to time, St. Augustine responded to those who asked why God created the world when he did and not before or after by pointing out that time itself is a creation. It can be detected only by change, and change requires created things. Such reasoning was also part of his rejection of 24-hour periods of creation, since in the first days, there was nothing in existence to mark time.

Others, like the 13th-century theologian and bishop Robert Grosseteste, reasoned that extension, the three-dimensions, was also a creation. Creation, if truly *ex nihilo*, did not fill up some preexisting emptiness. So Grosseteste concluded that time, space, matter, and light had to have been created in the initial moment of the *fiat lux*, let there be light. Following reason and the known principles of light, the known properties of light, Grosseteste reasoned that the natural radial propagation of light thus formed a spherical cosmos by its natural motion outward from an initial infinitesimal point of God's creative activity, generating dimensions as it went.

The unacceptable position was that of an eternal universe, a universe without beginning. Aristotle held this view, and his doctrine was rejected as untenable at the University of Paris by the famous Condemnation of 1277, a decree issued by the bishop of Paris. Despite various thoughts about creation, including exactly what "day" in Genesis I might mean, the age of the universe still remained small. In accordance with homocentric assumptions, why should there be an earth without man or a universe without an earth?

Now let's move to the 20th century. In the 20th century, there was a 40-year debate between two rival cosmologies that posited very different, in fact infinitely different, ages for the universe. These two cosmologies came to be known as the steady-state model and the "Big Bang" model. Both had theological ramifications. Let's compare what happened with them.

First, the Big Bang model—the name "Big Bang," I have to say, first of all, is a term of ridicule that was coined by the model's most boisterous opponent. It was initially called the "primordial atom" model, in 1927, by Georges Lemaître, a Belgian priest. Now Lemaître himself would consider his profession as a priest irrelevant to his scientific work, but it bears mentioning here for anyone tempted to forget that people in professed religious orders continue to do advanced scientific work down to the present day. After Lemaître's ordination in 1923, he studied mathematics and physics at Cambridge, Harvard, and then received a PhD from MIT before he returned to Belgium to become a professor at the University of Louvain.

Lemaître proposed his theory to explain a problem in Einsteinian relativity that predicted the universe should be either expanding or contracting. Einstein himself had added a fudge factor to his calculations to keep things stable. Scientists of the time simply expected the universe to be stable, to be eternal, to be unchanging. Lemaître instead proposed that the universe was not actually stable, that it was in fact expanding and therefore that it had a beginning in what he called a "single quantum." The explosion of this quantum generated time, space, and the universe. Initially, the idea was rejected. Some, including Einstein, felt that it sounded a little too much like Christian dogma.

Here's an interesting twist on the science-religion interaction: discomfort with a scientific theory now in the 20th century because it sounds too much like orthodox Christianity. In fact, it does uphold the Christian dogma of a cosmos beginning with a *creatio ex nihilo*, or at least beginning with the *ex nihilo* part, or at least the beginning part at the lowest possible level. Einstein himself, however, was won over after further conversations with Lemaître and called the idea, "the most beautiful and satisfactory explanation of creation to which I have ever listened."

In 1951, Pope Pius XII spoke in glowing terms of the Big Bang cosmology. The endorsement actually chagrined Lemaître. He had received a lot of criticism that his theory was religiously motivated, especially being a priest. And so he'd been struggling for 20 years to keep the science separate from any kind of theological ramifications. So he wasn't actually thrilled that the pope decided to endorse his theory.

You may know that Copernicus received the first copy of his *De revolutionibus* just shortly before he died. Just before Lemaître died in 1966, he received news of the detection of what is called the cosmic background radiation, the echoes of the primordial explosion that were predicted in his theory. This discovery won over the remaining critics, except for one, its loudest, Fred Hoyle, the one who coined the derisive term "Big Bang." Hoyle supported a steady-state model, an eternal universe. Its expansion, which by now had been observed by Edwin Hubble and others, was explained by the sudden but continual appearance of individual hydrogen atoms, a few here, a few there. Hoyle himself was vociferously anti-religious and especially anti-clerical, particularly, I might add, anti-Catholic. He in fact advocated solving the troubles in Northern Ireland by imprisoning all priests for life. He rarely missed a chance to assail traditional belief and to ridicule the seeming affinity of the Big Bang with it.

Yet ironically, while he linked his own steady-state model to an atheistic campaign, others were able to interpret it theologically. Although it violated the letter of the eternity criterion, the steady appearance of hydrogen atoms from empty space was read by some as a continuing *creatio ex nihilo*, evidence of God's continuing activity in the physical world. Well look at that; it's exactly the sort of thing that 17th-century natural philosophers like Boyle and Newton had been looking for. Thus, we see again the potential flexibility of scientific ideas to theological interpretation.

Lemaître's Big Bang is now the accepted cosmological model, and it would be difficult not to see here a place where a theological doctrine—in fact, the only strict dogma relating to physical creation in orthodox Christianity—was upheld against a once prevailing scientific view. Don't take me wrong, I am not indulging in apologetics here. I am only pointing out one counterexample to claims that when theological and scientific perspectives are at odds, theology is always the loser. Of course, here theology's win, if we can even call it that, was achieved through scientific studies carried out by priests, believers, agnostics, and atheists, once again, nicely complicating the picture.

What we've seen in this lecture are steady increases to the age of the earth and the age and size of the universe. This progressively undercut medieval homocentric perceptions—man's dominion was made ever smaller in time and space and his cosmological centrality was lost. Even though these scientific discoveries did not oppose any orthodox dogmas, contrary to popular opinion, they did have a direct impact on standard assumptions, and thereby on theological discussions.

Many religious people have taken man's new position as a lesson in humility and celebrate a divine creativity of much greater extent than ever before imagined. And that's the central issue of this lecture, that scientific findings and theories have proven remarkably malleable to theologians, open to multiple interpretations. The diversity of theological responses to scientific ideas shows the falseness of the claim that theology has historically simply opposed scientific development. In every instance, some theologians or religious individuals have been naysayers, but at least as many have embraced new ideas to see what new things they might imply about the world, God, and God's relation to it.

In our next lecture, we are going to take up a development whose way was cleared by the new age of the earth, perhaps the most celebrated of all the science-religion issues: Darwinian evolution.

Lecture Ten
Darwin and Responses to Evolution

Scope:

Like Galileo, Charles Darwin occupies a central position in discussions of science and religion. This lecture looks at Darwin's theory of evolution and its complex reception in context. Although evolutionary ideas were already a topic of popular discussion in England, Darwin's natural selection and common ancestry ideas impinged upon several key theological issues. Most importantly, they provoked a wide range of responses from different religious and scientific figures. Not only could Darwinian ideas be used for diametrically opposed purposes, but also (contrary to common rhetoric), by the end of the century, many mainstream Christian thinkers had incorporated evolution (if not natural selection) into their religious views.

Outline

I. In 1859, Charles Darwin published his epochal *Origin of Species*; this was followed in 1871 by *The Descent of Man*. The responses, scientific and theological, were complex.

    A. Three important features of Darwin's evolutionary principles were common ancestry, speciation through variation, and natural selection.

        1. *Common ancestry* holds that all species in existence today originate from a single ancient organism or a very small number of ancient organisms.

        2. Species come about through the *variation* of forms, organs, and instincts; these variations are random.

        3. *Natural selection* is the mechanism for speciation; useful variations promote survival and favor reproduction and are, thus, passed on to more progeny. In other words, useful variations are "selected for."

        4. Herbert Spencer referred to this last as "survival of the fittest."

    B. It must be remembered that Darwin presented his ideas during a time of wider intellectual crisis, in which several related developments were ongoing.

1. The "age of the Earth" issue was continuing, and higher criticism was a subject of hot controversy.
2. Evolutionary thinking about the natural world, moreover, was not new.
3. The sciences were now completing their professionalization, and part of this process was the exclusion of pronouncements on origins, purposes, and ultimate meanings.

II. Darwin's ideas could have an impact on theology in many ways—many of which we have encountered in other contexts.

A. There was an impact on biblical authority, specifically in terms of the historicity of Genesis 1.
1. Thus, theologians and others who held to strict interpretations of the Bible tended to reject Darwin's ideas.
2. This, however, was not the main source of contention in the 19th century.

B. The argument from design, upon which so much English religious apologetic had been built, was undermined by the notion of random variations and natural selection.
1. Indeed, Paley's 1802 book was an argument that adaptation indicated design, rather than a response to environmental changes, as proposed by Lamarck and others.
2. The old problem of God's activity in the world was renewed if species can develop naturally without the need for special creation (that is, individual production by God).
3. With the design argument undermined by random variation, atheism was again an issue—no superintendence, no God. The Princeton Presbyterian theologian Charles Hodge (1797–1878) thus equated Darwinism with atheism.

C. On an ethical level, both the distancing of God and the notion of "survival of the fittest" were seen as undercutting morality in human relations. A nature run by violent, brutal natural selection could not witness a merciful, benevolent God or instantiate morality.

D. The origin of man from lower organisms was potentially materialistic, if exception were not made for the soul.

  1. Materialism was a tumultuous movement on the Continent; ideas of German materialists undergirded radical politics (for example, the politics of Karl Marx) and attacks on Christianity.

  2. German materialists, such as Ernst Haeckel (1834–1919) and David Friedrich Strauss (1808–1874), adopted evolution specifically to further their attacks on religion.

  3. Materialism was explicitly condemned by the First Vatican Council in 1870.

E. Some found the "lower origins" of man undignified or unsuitable for the *imago Dei.* Yet others, such as the Baptist A. H. Strong (1836–1921)—even though a biblical conservative—argued that humans are no less human even if evolved from beasts.

III. Contrary to much mythology, religious leaders were significantly divided in their reception to Darwinism.

  A. Although some argued that it undermined Christianity, many others saw evolution as consistent with a divine plan and even as *proof* of divine purpose in the world.

   1. A necessary background is Robert Chambers's *Vestiges of a Natural History of Creation* (1844), which envisioned a plan "programmed into" creation by God at the beginning.

   2. Even Thomas Henry Huxley ("Darwin's bulldog") initially expressed reservations about evolution because it seemed too progressivist and, thus, religious.

   3. A sense of progress still spoke to purpose and design (in his later years, Darwin rejected progressivism) and fit nicely with Victorian social and political ideas of "progress."

  B. The use of Darwin's ideas could be completely dimorphic.

   1. Some found in Darwin support for the biblical teaching that all mankind had a common ancestor (*monogenism*).

   2. But others used it to support *polygenism* (multiple origins of humanity), which in turn, supported racism and colonialism through "survival of the fittest."

C. Religious motives sometimes played a role in *spreading* evolution.

  1. Liberal theologians were anxious to distinguish themselves from conservatives who stuck to biblical literalism.

  2. Contrariwise, there has been, throughout the 20th century, a tendency for some less educated Protestants to assert and reinforce religious identity through opposition to evolution more than through theological principles.

D. Catholics, who tended to be neither biblical literalists nor wedded to the argument from design, were concerned primarily about the danger of materialism.

  1. Saint George Mivart (1827–1900), an anatomist, opposed natural selection as the mechanism for evolution in favor of theistic evolution.

  2. In 1950, Pius XII gave conditional support to evolution, and in 1996, John Paul II declared it "more than a hypothesis."

  3. At the same time, both popes continued the Church's opposition to materialistic interpretations; the soul exists and is not a product of evolution.

IV. By the 1890s, there was nearly universal acceptance of the concept of biological evolution (transformation of species) but little for natural selection as the mechanism.

  A. Most interpreters of Genesis had settled on the *Day-Age theory* or *Gap theory*.

  1. According to the Day-Age theory, each of the six days of creation represented a vast geological epoch.

  2. According to the Gap theory, there was a vast period of time between the creation of heaven and Earth and the rest of creation.

  B. Many theologians and scientists embraced *theistic evolution*, the idea that God guides or directs evolution.

  1. This system was worked out extensively by Darwin's American proponent, the Harvard botanist Asa Gray, and was adopted (in the case of humans) by Alfred Russell Wallace, the independent originator of natural selection.

  2. Within theistic evolution, the level of God's involvement can span a very broad range.

C. The diversity of responses to and reworkings of Darwinian theory by theologians and religious scientists forbids the making of facile, sweeping generalizations about the interaction between evolution and Christian thought.

Essential Reading:

Lindberg and Numbers, *God and Nature*, chapter 15 (pp. 369–390).

John Paul II, "Address to Pontifical Academy of Sciences," 22 October 1996.

Supplementary Reading:

Brooke, *Science and Religion*, chapter 8 (pp. 275–320).

Questions to Consider:

1. Polygenism (and, to a lesser extent, Darwinian evolution itself) was used by some to justify slavery and racism. To what extent is it reasonable to oppose a scientific idea, theory, or development on the grounds that it leads to ethically objectionable positions? Can you think of other examples?

2. Consider the Day-Age theory and Gap theory (as well as St. Augustine's exegesis). How do we know where to start and stop in interpretations of Scripture? What are the messages that Christians need to preserve from Genesis 1? Consider arguments for the varying degrees of literalism as applied to Genesis 1 (or to the rest of Scripture).

Lecture Ten—Transcript
Darwin and Responses to Evolution

The most active and controversial issue in the science-religion relationship nowadays is certainly that of evolution. I am sure there's been much more ink spilled about this one topic than all the rest of the science-religion controversy put together. It remains a topic that evokes emotional responses and I should say, to equal degrees, on both sides of the issue. Unfortunately, emotion tends to put reason to flight, and in this case, we are in greater need of reason than emotion.

In this lecture, we are going to speed through the major points of Darwin's theory and contextualize them in relationship to currents in science-theology conversations of the time. We will also survey reactions to Darwinian evolution down to the end of the 19th century. In the next lecture, we will move onto the 20th century to focus specifically on reactions in 20th-century America, particularly in relationship to the rise of fundamentalism.

Without further ado, let's review the main features of Darwin's evolutionary theory. Charles Darwin proposed the major features of his evolutionary theory in two books, in the *Origin of Species*, published in 1859, which was followed some years later, in 1871, by *The Descent of Man*. There are three basic features to Darwin's proposal.

First, common ancestry—this holds that all species originated from one or a small number of ancient organisms. Now a lot of the emotional impact of Darwinism originates here because human beings are included in the evolutionary tree. The fact that this is a raw nerve is revealed by the tendency of critics, both in the 19th century and down to the present day, to make indignant exclamations about people coming from apes, a claim of course which is not made by Darwinians who actually posit a common ancestor, neither ape nor human, from which both apes and human beings descend.

Second is the concept of variation by mutation; this deals with how new species arise from old ones, namely, the forms, organs, and instincts of an individual can differ in small and random ways from those of its progenitor, and that these new characteristics can be passed on to the next generation. This point proved far less controversial.

The third point is natural selection as the mechanism of speciation. Although there may be any number of variations, they are not all equally passed on to the next generation. Variations which prove to be useful adaptations that promote an individual's survival will thereby enhance reproduction and so are passed on to a larger number of offspring. In this way, useful variations are selected for. This point was hotly debated both in science and in theology. It was also translated out of the biological realm and into the social realm by Herbert Spencer and others, as Spencer cited it under the slightly misleading motto of "survival of the fittest." More about that problem in a few minutes.

Now some contextualization. The second half of the 19th century was a period of enormous upheavals, socially, intellectually, technologically, and politically. I am going to have to restrict myself because of time considerations just to the intellectual ones. Two issues we treated last time are of particular importance. First, the age of the earth was still being debated. There were still Mosaicists writing popular books, in particular, even though geology had become by this point a thoroughly professionalized field. The age of the earth is crucial since Darwin's mechanism of speciation would require a very old earth, certainly much longer than the 6,000 or so years of Mosaicists.

Second, higher criticism remained a very hot topic of controversy, particularly in England, and it was something that clearly distinguished different theologians into different classes. Finally, I have to stress that evolution was not a new topic in 1859. What's new in Darwin's case is specifically the mechanism of natural selection. Evolutionary changes and variations had been talked about since the 18th century. In fact, Charles Darwin's grandfather, Erasmus Darwin, was involved in these early discussions.

The 1840s and 50s saw heightened awareness of the topic, even on a popular level, thanks to a very controversial book in the natural theology tradition called *Vestiges of a Natural History of Creation*, published anonymously in 1844. The *Vestiges* proposed, in a very engaging popular style—it's an easy book to read—that evolutionary development of the world was the natural course of things. This author, eventually identified as Robert Chambers, wrote, "All of creation developed gradually in accordance with natural law." But the natural world was not the only place for evolutionary thinking.

The intellectual and political world embraced evolution as well. I will remind you only of August Comte's three stages of human intellectual development, so beloved by John William Draper. So Darwinism appeared on an already turbulent scene, one deeply interested in, concerned about, and divided over many of the topics that Darwin would highlight.

Darwin's ideas impinge on several theological issues, most of which we've already encountered in other contexts. The simplest instance—Darwinism had an impact on biblical authority, specifically in terms of interpretations of Genesis I—nothing new there. Thus, those who held to strict, that is, more directly literal interpretations of the Bible, tended to reject Darwin's ideas. What is striking and what I have to emphasize is that, in the 19th century, this was the weakest objection and the one, it may surprise you to hear, most easily overcome.

Much more problematic was what the idea of random variation and natural selection did to a tradition that was by now thoroughly entrenched in English-speaking culture, namely, natural theology and the argument from design. This foundation upon which English religious apologetic had been built for almost two centuries was undermined by the notion of random variations and natural selection. In short, the awe-inspiring anatomical features, rather than being exquisite contrivances that bore witness to divine design and wisdom, were now to be seen as the cumulative product of eons of minute, random variations selected naturally and statistically by environmental pressures and more successful reproduction. In short, what we sense as design is in fact a natural result of inherent natural processes, like the fact that all the planets and satellites revolve and rotate in the same direction or the intricate structure of snowflakes.

So we're back at an old problem, the problem of God's activity in nature. If new species can develop naturally and without the need for special creation—that is, individual production by the hand of God—then here's another place where God's direct action is not needed. In other words, the natural theologian's god of the gaps was being squeezed out of yet another closing gap, and a very big one in fact. Thus Darwinism threatened English religious apologetic with progressive collapse. If random variation and natural selection undermined arguments from design, that weakened in turn natural theology, which had been supporting the bulk of English apologetics for the existence of God.

Thus fear about atheism became again an issue via fear of the argument: no design, no God. This concern came out most straightforwardly in the 1874 book by the Princeton Presbyterian theologian, Charles Hodge, entitled *What is Darwinism?* Towards the end of his book, Hodge answered the question bluntly: "Darwinism is atheism." Significantly, Hodge came to this conclusion largely on the basis of the impact of Darwinism for natural theology. He found it, "absolutely impossible to believe that the eye is not a work of design and, further, denial of design in nature is virtually the denial of God."

Hodge's theology envisioned a god working directly in the world. He was not satisfied with distancing God from creation via a chain of secondary causes. What kind of a position is this? Do you remember? This is a supernaturalist position. God is exerting his direct action on the world all the time rather than having delegated powers to natural things.

I know that we should always be very wary of conjectural history. By conjectural history, I mean "what if" history, how could things have turned out differently. But in this case, I think it's fairly safe to conjecture that if the English-speaking world had not built up so large a tradition of natural theology for almost two centuries and had not come to rely upon it so heavily for the single proposition of God's existence, then natural selection would not have provoked so strong a religious response.

We can adduce in support of this claim the fact that the reception of Darwin outside of England and America, where natural theology had far less currency and importance, was quite different. The theological issue that was particularly troubling on the continent was the danger of materialism. Remember we spoke about materialism when we were talking about the mechanical philosophy. It's the idea that everything can be explained in terms of matter and motion, and the concern that this left no room for spiritual entities that are at the center of religion, God and the soul.

In the present case of evolution, the origin of man from lower organisms by natural processes was potentially materialistic unless exception was made for the creation and infusion of the human soul.

Materialism had already grown into a tumultuous movement on the continent by 1859. The ideas particularly of German materialists undergirded radical politics, most notably those of Karl Marx. And this radical politics, in its assault on the established political order, also included strident materialist attacks on Christianity, which was of course allied with the established political order.

The support evolution gave to materialist thinking was actually a factor in its acceptance by some. One example is the German biologist Ernst Haeckel, although he did not accept Darwin's mechanism of natural selection. Indeed, Haeckel is the most strident atheist that we have yet encountered. In 1877, he wrote:

> The cell consists of protoplasm, composed chiefly of carbon with an admixture of hydrogen, nitrogen, and sulfur. These component parts, properly nursed, become man. With this single argument, the mystery of the universe is explained, the deity annulled, and a new era of infinite knowledge ushered in."

Wow! There you have it all: materialism, atheism, scientism, all wrapped up with astonishing arrogance. We will have more to say about this blend of notions in our concluding lecture.

For now, Haeckel's bold claims illustrate the problems we're talking about and make it clear why materialism was one of the philosophical positions condemned as an error by Pius IX and again, a few years later in 1870, by the First Vatican Council. Finally, in terms of emotional impact if not necessarily in terms of rational theology, many people objected to the common origins theory for man because they found the lower animal origins undignified and unsuitable for the being created in God's image.

Still, some religious leaders did not find this a problem. One example is A.H. Strong, an American Baptist, and one strongly on the conservative side in terms of biblical authority and interpretation. He argued in his 1886 book *Systematic Theology* that humans are no less human even if evolved from beasts. "Just as," he says, "the wine that Christ produced from water at the marriage in Cana is no less wine for having once been water,"—beautiful comparison there.

Perhaps the most important point about evolution that early 21st-century listeners should know is this: 19th-century religious leaders and theologians expressed almost every conceivable response to

Darwinian evolution. It would also be a gross mistake to think that theologians and scientists divided up into opposite camps based on Darwinism. Theologians and scientists both were scattered from one end of the spectrum to the other in their responses to Darwinism. Some religious leaders, like Hodge, did see evolution as undermining Christianity. And we've just seen how some materialists explicitly used it for just such a purpose. That's one end of the spectrum.

But a great number of religious leaders saw the general concept of evolution as consistent with a divine plan, and some saw it even as proof of a divine purpose. In other words, evolutionary schemes could be summed up and put into a new kind of natural theology. The necessary background to all of this is the book I mentioned a few minute's ago, *Vestiges of a Natural History of Creation*, published in 1844, 15 years before *Origin of Species*. The book envisioned a progressive evolutionary plan that was programmed into creation by God at the beginning. The world was evolving, all according to a providential divine blueprint that had been encased in natural laws. For some, there might have been theological problems with determinism here. But the *Vestiges* brought a theistic version of evolutionary thinking to a very wide public.

A sense of progress in nature spoke to ultimate purpose and design. Now Darwin, in his later years, rejected progressivism, that is, that evolution means constant advancement. But this, in fact, others said, was hard to argue from the fossil record, which by and large shows more advanced forms later in time. The idea of progress in nature harmonized beautifully with Victorian ideas of social and political progress as well. So there's a harmony here with the idea of evolution and ideas in the wider culture, including religious culture.

Now Darwin's ideas were co-opted by a wide range of thinkers, and may I say, they then evolved into new forms by being subjected to new environments and new pressures. They could be used, just as we saw in the last lecture in terms of age of the earth, to support completely opposite points of view. Here is an example. The principle of common ancestry, in variation, argues for the emergence of a first man—the first creature able to be called "human"—from who all later humans are thereby descended. This view is known as monogenism, single origin, such if you can support biblical teaching that all mankind is related through Adam. It thus can undergird, for example, the doctrine of original sin and, by direct consequence, that of universal redemption through Christ. It could also undergird the fundamental Christian moral principle that all men are brothers and thus the ethical, moral, and behavioral obligations that flow from that idea.

Yet, others used the very same principles to argue that humanity had several origins through several original human beings, evolved in different parts of the world. A position of polygenism, many origins. Now look where this idea, which by the way was formally condemned by the Catholic Church and many Protestant theologians, where will it lead? When combined with Social Darwinism, Spencer's "survival of the fittest," polygenism gives a scientific justification for racism and colonialism. This was a useful perspective, by the way, for business and political interests at the time who were benefiting from England's imperial expansion in the 19th century, just as Haeckel's declaration that politics is applied biology was co-opted 20 years after his death to justify Nazi race policies. In the American South, polygenism was called to support the institution of slavery.

Another surprising notion is that sometimes religious motives played a positive role in accepting and spreading evolution. That may sound like quite a surprising statement. But some liberal theologians— those who embraced higher criticism, for example—were anxious to distinguish themselves from conservatives and evangelicals who stuck to biblical literalism. So acceptance of evolutionary thinking generally modified, in one way or another, could be a way to define a particular intellectual and social group among Christian theologians. In other words, by accepting evolution, you put yourself in a particular group and separate yourself from another group that you don't want to be associated with.

Acceptance of evolution could be a mark to indicate that you are a modern and enlightened theologian. In 20th-century America, we can easily see just the same social phenomenon happening in reverse. Remember, you can never define just one group. Defining one group always defines two; drawing a line of demarcation marks an inside and an outside. So through the 20th century, there has been a tendency for the less educated, often less formally educated, to assert and reinforce religious identity through opposition to evolution. Opposition to evolution becomes in effect a badge of membership. Indeed, some recent American sects define themselves in practice as much through opposition to evolution as by adherence to any specific theological doctrine.

So far, we've dealt almost entirely with Protestant responses. Catholic responses provide further possibilities for the engagement of theology with evolution. Protestants, as we've seen, tended to worry about the conflict with literal readings of scripture to some extent, but more about the implications for natural theology and the argument from design. Catholics, on the other hand, who tended in general to be neither biblical literalists nor wedded to a natural theology tradition and its argument from design in the way that English Protestants were, responded in different ways. Catholic responses tended to be more muted, and they were directed primarily against materialism and polygenism. The key points for discussion among Catholic theologians thus were, and in fact remain to the present day, the divine origin of the human soul and the consanguinity of the human race.

One early response from a Catholic scientist—actually he was a convert to Catholicism in England—was the *Genesis of Species* by Saint George Mivart. I should say, Saint George is his first name, he is not canonized, that is just his first name. He was an anatomist. He, like so many scientists of the day, opposed natural selection as the mechanism of evolution even while accepting biological evolution in general. He propounded a theistic view of evolution, bearing some resemblances to what was set forth in the *Vestiges*—namely, that the evolutionary process was divinely guided in one way or another.

For him, God had established laws of development that evolving organisms follow. As evidence, he pointed to separate evolutionary lines—that is, separate lines of descent through different groups of organisms—that showed similar progression occurring independently, implying for him that they were guided by some yet unknown natural law, rather than by chance variations and natural selection, which would not be expected to produce similar anatomical changes in different organisms in different situations. Moreover, he explicitly noted that the soul was an immaterial entity and could not be a product of evolution.

The hardening of some Protestant positions against evolution in the early 20th century that we will talk about next time did not have a counterpart among Catholics. Indeed, Catholics remained largely silent during the heated arguments of the teens and twenties we will survey this next time. But in 1950, Pope Pius XII, in his encyclical *Humani Generis* ("Of the Human Race"), allowed for discussions of evolution between theologians and scientists, but at the same time noted that while it was certainly praiseworthy for the church to take into account as much as possible demonstrated scientific knowledge, evolution remained at that point a hypothesis. Does that sound familiar? Well it should. It's the same cautious sentiment that we've heard from Saints Augustine and Bellarmino regarding science and theology. Pius XII also took the opportunity in this encyclical to note that evolution can regard only the origin of the human body, not the soul.

A more recent and celebrated statement was that of John Paul II in 1996. Here he reiterated opposition to materialistic interpretations: the soul exists and is not a product of evolution. But he also updated Pius XII's comments:

> Today, almost half a century after the publication of the encyclical *Humani Generis*, new knowledge has led to the recognition of the theory of evolution as more than a hypothesis. It is indeed remarkable that this theory has been progressively accepted by researchers following a series of discoveries in various fields of knowledge. The convergence, neither sought nor fabricated, of the results of work that was conducted independently is, in itself, a significant argument in favor of this theory.

Note the careful use of proper philosophical terminology. John Paul was after all a professor of philosophy. Evolution is no longer a hypothesis. Well, what's a hypothesis? It is a provisional statement, a supposition in the process of being tested. But John Paul calls evolution a theory. Is that something different? Yes it is, even if it's not necessarily so in common parlance. There is a big difference. The word "theory," properly used, does not mean a guess or a supposition. Often people contrast theory and fact, as in the dismissive statement, "Oh, that's just a theory." But that is incorrect. A theory is not something waiting to be proven, to grow up into a fact. A theory is something far greater than a fact could ever be. A theory is a well-supported explanatory structure capable of explaining and predicting a range of phenomena. A fact is just an isolated tidbit of knowledge, but a theory organizes facts, concepts, and predictions into a functional, scientific framework. So, for example, the theory of gravity explains and predicts planetary motions, projectile motions, and falling apples. But no one says, "The theory of gravity is just a theory."

What John Paul II was actually doing was updating Pius XII's statement. Evidence accumulated in the intervening 50 years between the two statements indicated that evolution now has the status of a theory, that is, a powerful organizational structure for biology. I will just point out that this really is exactly the kind of thing that St. Augustine was asking for back in his *De Genesi ad litteram*, the literal commentary on Genesis, that once scientific knowledge progresses, we have to adjust our biblical interpretations, our theology, to accommodate it.

Back to the 19th century. The 30 years following *Origin of Species* was a time full of discussions and divergent positions in theology and science in regard to evolution. The most hostile responses were particularly the early ones. By the 1880s, a shift was apparent and that was a shift towards accommodation. By the end of the century, there was nearly universal acceptance, by both scientists and theologians, of the concept of biological evolution in terms of the transformation of species, but considerably less for natural selection as its mechanism. Viewed from 1900, Darwin had been wildly successful in advancing the general concept of evolution, but ironically enough, was less successful in promoting his own particular contribution to the topic, that is, natural selection.

Most conflicts with Genesis had been solved. By century's end, many theologians had adopted higher criticism, which read Genesis I as a creation myth containing spiritual truths but in a highly poetic language. Most who did not adopt higher criticism had settled on the "Day-Age" or "Gap" Theory. We met the Day-Age Theory last time. It holds that each of the six days of creation represents a vast geological epoch. The Gap Theory allows for the insertion of vast period of time between the days. Thus the vast age of the earth was no longer an issue if you are a gap theorist.

In terms of the fear of atheism or materialism, by the end of the century, many of these concerns had been allayed by the concept of a theistic evolution. That means that evolution was a natural process guided or directed in some way by God. But note, theistic evolution was not some watered-down version of evolution—it wasn't evolution-light for theologians—it was developed by scientists and widely accepted by scientists who, remember, then as now, were just as likely to be theists anyway. Theistic evolution was worked out extensively by one of Darwin's major American proponents, the Harvard botanist Asa Gray, who concluded that variation has been led along certain beneficial lines. Gray's system was politely rejected by Darwin himself. Yet theistic versions of evolution proved very powerful, being adopted by many, including, for the case of human development, by Alfred Russell Wallace, the independent originator of natural selection.

We've already talked about different positions regarding the level of God's involvement in the natural world. Theistic evolution recapitulates these different positions, that is to say, the level of God's involvement with the evolutionary process could span a very large range. At the most naturalistic end, after God's initial creative act, evolution just proceeded naturally to form man's body, which once complete, God put a human soul into.

This lecture brings us to the end of the 19th century. In our next lecture, we are going to continue looking at responses to evolution, but in the 20th century, particularly in the context of that peculiarly American construction, fundamentalism.

Lecture Eleven
Fundamentalism and Creationism

Scope:

Despite the wide acceptance of evolutionary ideas by naturalists and prominent theologians in 1900, the 20th century has been marked by the strongest ever science-religion conflict in regard to evolution. The 1925 Scopes Monkey Trial, famed in popular imagination, on stage, and in film, was a highpoint in the 1920s fundamentalist crusade against evolution. In fact, the trial was part setup, part publicity stunt, although it soon ran out of control. This lecture looks not only at the Scopes Trial but also at its successors, as well as the invention of creation science and flood geology. Also important here is a brief analysis of the historical background and social (anxiety) foundations of American fundamentalism, a force that continues to play a largely adversarial role with modern science.

Outline

I. In the United States, recent science-religion issues have most often involved the opposition of fundamentalists to science and scientists.

    A. Surprisingly, there is more opposition to evolution and other scientific topics in the United States today than there was at the end of the 19th century.

        1. By 1900, most American clergy had accommodated some form of an ancient Earth and evolution into their beliefs.

        2. The rise of fundamentalism would change this situation within a generation.

    B. Fundamentalism as a movement began in the early 20th century.

        1. The name derives from a set of 12 tracts, *The Fundamentals*, published in 1910–1915.

        2. Fundamentalism contains an aggregate of beliefs, including naïve literalism, biblical inerrancy, and the residuals of 19th-century millenarist sects.

3. Nineteenth-century millenarianism undergirds the first two beliefs; 19th-century America was awash with prophets of doom, predicting the apocalypse. The roots of this movement lay in dispensational millennialism, a new 19th-century notion that there were seven ages to human history marked by different ways—*dispensations*—that God tried to deal with humanity. Millenarians believed they were living in the sixth age, soon to be followed by an age of tribulation—the millennium. They wanted to determine exactly when the millennium would begin.

4. Millenarianism gave rise to many apocalyptic beliefs and movements, including the continuing fundamentalist obsession with the New Testament Book of Revelation.

5. Thus, naïve literalism and biblical inerrancy became a natural consequence of millenarianism, given its preoccupation with calculating dates from specific biblical passages.

6. Fundamentalism is as much a social as a religious movement; its views are group-defining.

7. Fundamentalism is a reactionary movement. Key stimuli are social anxiety over the loss of the old order (a religiously oriented Anglo-Saxon Protestant America) and fear of perceived foes: urban and learned culture, modernity, intellectuals, industrialization, immigration, and so on.

8. Accordingly, its origins overlap those of the second Ku Klux Klan.

C. The fundamentalists' "hot-button" issues have changed over time.
1. Initial opposition was largely to higher criticism; even evolution was treated benignly in *The Fundamentals*.

2. The explosion of fundamentalist belligerency dates from the period of World War I and its aftermath.

3. The enormous growth of public high schools in the period 1900–1920 exposed rural populations to modern science; thus, evolution became a key issue.

4. Since that time, other reactionary issues have been added, for example, opposition to the civil rights movement, women's rights, and so on.

II. Fundamentalists gained wide exposure in the famous Scopes Monkey Trial of 1925.

    A. Contrary to dramatic depictions in film and on stage (*Inherit the Wind*), the trial was actually a setup.

    B. Tennessee, under fundamentalist pressures, passed a law (the Butler Act) in 1925 banning the teaching of evolution.

        1. The ACLU sought a test case.

        2. The town leaders of Dayton asked a teacher, John T. Scopes, if he was willing to stand as a defendant in order to provide a case; he agreed.

        3. Town leaders hoped that the trial would bring publicity and visitors (with money) to a struggling town.

        4. The result was as much circus as trial.

    C. Big guns showed up for the legal team: William Jennings Bryan for the prosecution and Clarence Darrow for the defense.

        1. Bryan had begun crusading against evolution in 1922; his influence was key in passing the Butler Act.

        2. He extended his populist credo in an aggressively anti-intellectual way to science.

        3. Nonetheless, his opposition to evolution was not solely demagoguery; it partly reflected his traditional messages of labor rights and human dignity, which he felt were imperiled by the common origins theory.

        4. The surprise drama occurred when Bryan took the stand and was made to appear a buffoon by Darrow.

    D. The trial was eventually restricted to the narrow question of whether or not Scopes broke the law; scientific and theological experts were not allowed to testify.

        1. Scopes, who never took the stand, was convicted and fined $100.

        2. This sentence was overturned on a technicality, preventing the case from reaching the Supreme Court.

    E. Fundamentalists receded from the scene after the 1920s, but evolution also receded from biology textbooks, owing to book publishers' concerns about sales.

III. After 30 years of dormancy, fundamentalist opposition to evolution returned in the 1960s.

    A. This return was sparked by improved secondary school education in the rural South and Midwest.

        1. Following Sputnik, improved science education was promoted at the federal level; one result, in 1963, was the Biological Sciences Curriculum Study (BSCS), which produced a massively improved high school biology textbook, containing evolution.

        2. This curriculum set off a new wave of attempts to ban evolution, but the old bans (in Arkansas) were overturned by the U. S. Supreme Court in 1968.

    B. After this failure, fundamentalists turned to the equal-time strategy. Thus, creation science was promoted as an alternative to evolution.

    C. Creationism can be difficult to discuss because an enormously wide range of distinct viewpoints can coexist under the name.

        1. *General* creationists affirm only in a nonspecific way that God is the ultimate creator, while *special* creationists assign God specific tasks.

        2. Special creationists are divided into *progressive* and *strict*; the former interpret the Bible allegorically, while the latter take it literally as a scientific text.

        3. Progressive creationists are yet further divided into those who limit God's actions to a single act or very few acts (for example, initiating life), and those who require a separate creative act for each species or genus.

        4. Strict creationists are likewise divided into those adhering to the Gap theory, who envision a long epoch before the six days, and the Young-Earth creationists, who consider the Earth less than 10,000 years old.

        5. Thus, when speaking of creationists, we have to be very careful to identify specific groups accurately.

    D. Creation science represented strict creationist views, generally of the Young-Earth sort; while it originated in the 1960s, its roots are older and based in *flood geology*.

1. In 1923, George McCready Price, a Seventh-Day Adventist, published *The New Geology*, which held that the strata and the fossil record were relics of Noah's Flood.
2. In 1961, *The Genesis Flood* by Henry M. Morris and John Whitcomb revived Price's claims.
3. One result was the founding of the Creation Science Society in 1963.
4. Initially successful equal-time arguments, however, were turned back in 1987 when the Supreme Court recognized creation science as religious doctrine, not science.

E. The next shift was to mask identifiably religious content in order to pass constitutional muster—the result was *neocreationism*, of which Abrupt Appearance theory and Intelligent Design form a part.

Essential Reading:

Edward J. Larson, *Summer for the Gods*.

Lindberg and Numbers, *God and Nature*, chapter 16 (pp. 391–423).

Supplementary Reading:

George M. Marsden, *Understanding Fundamentalism and Evangelicalism*.

Questions to Consider:

1. It has been suggested that in modern America, the so-called battle between science and religion is, in fact, a face-off between learned/elite science and religion and unlearned/"popular" science and religion. Consider this interpretation and come up with evidence for and/or against it.

2. What is a *shibboleth*? (And where does the word come from?) It has been remarked that opposition to evolution is a *shibboleth* (rather than a rationally held belief) for many fundamentalists. Consider this suggestion and see if you can identify *shibboleths* for scientistic opponents of fundamentalist anti-evolutionism.

Lecture Eleven—Transcript
Fundamentalism and Creationism

One reason the issues of science and religion command such attention at present is their timeliness. Stories appear fairly regularly in the popular press dealing with the interactions, generally not cooperative ones, between science and religion at the present day in America. Most stories deal with the continuing responses to evolution from American Fundamentalists. So this lecture will be about the origins and features of these current events.

What we are going to do is survey the genesis of Fundamentalism in the early 20th century and examine the famous "Scopes Monkey Trial." We will then follow some more recent legal battles and analyze creation science. I need to start this lecture by stressing that there is more religiously motivated opposition to evolution in the United States today than there was at the start of the 20th century.

By 1900, evolution as a concept—if not natural selection as a mechanism—had gained wide acceptance in both scientific and theological circles. A large and steadily increasing proportion of American clergy, from Episcopalians to Evangelicals, had accommodated some form of the ancient earth and biological evolution into their theologies. Viewed from 1900, the trend was clear, namely, that naïvely literal readings of Genesis, such as a literal six-day creation and a special creation for each individual species, were quickly becoming things of the past.

Yet, something happened. By 1920, naïve literalism and the opposition to biological evolution had roared back to life in America with a prominence and a belligerence never before seen. The cause was the rise of Fundamentalism, and it changed everything within a generation. How did this happen and why? Let's begin with the origins of Fundamentalism.

Fundamentalism as a movement began in the early 20th century as an essentially American product. The name "Fundamentalism" derives from a set of 12 tracts, called *The Fundamentals*, published from 1910 to 1915 under the editorship of A.C. Dixon, a Baptist leader. These paperback volumes were mass produced and widely distributed. They shared an emphasis on conservative doctrine and an opposition to modernism. Now modernism is a movement towards new theological perspectives in Protestantism, particularly manifested in Episcopalian and in northern Methodist churches. Higher criticism, a key feature of modernism, came in for particular attack. Thus, Fundamentalism, from its origins, is inherently a reactionary movement.

The edges of Fundamentalism are quite hazy, simply because one could be a Fundamentalist and belong to a number of different denominations. It was Southern Baptists and Presbyterians and especially lesser local Bible sects that responded most avidly to the call of "The Fundamentals." We can divide Fundamentalist beliefs into two groups, the theological and the sociopolitical, and the two are inextricably linked. First, the theological. I think there are three interlocking features that are most important: naïve literalism, biblical inerrancy, and 19th-century millenarianism.

Let's take the last one first because it explains and undergirds the other two. Nineteenth-century America was awash with prophets of doom. Itinerant preachers and self-styled prophets clamored incessantly about an impending apocalypse. It's a chapter in American history that we almost always forget about. It's not generally covered in the political history of the U.S., but it was a very important movement in the 19th century.

Groups of believers banded together to await the end. And precise predictions of its date were very common. One example were the Millerites, followers of William Miller, a Baptist farmer from Upstate New York. They expected the end in 1843, and that was later revised to the 22nd of October, 1844. The roots of this movement lay in the invention of dispensational millennialism. Dispensational millennialism was a then novel notion that there were seven ages to human history, marked by different ways— dispensations—that God tried to deal with humanity. Currently, we live in the sixth age, the age of grace. But soon, supposedly, that will end, and the last age will begin—a final period full of tribulation called "The Millennium," hence millenarianism or millennialism.

The need was to determine exactly when the millennium would begin. So millennialists of the 19th century began frantic calculations based on numbers and prophecies in the Bible. The continuing effect of this 19th-century largely American development are enormous. It's the local source for apocalyptic utterances in everything from headlines in the weekly world news to bad Hollywood films about the antichrist. From this source arose also the strange notion of the

Rapture, which has become popular, that the supposed faithful would suddenly disappear at the start of the millennium, a belief totally unheard of before the 19th century.

Likewise, here begins the origin of continuing Fundamentalist emphasis on the New Testament Book of Revelations, a document not even universally accepted as canonical until the 16th century. Given the centrality of calculating dates from specific biblical passages, you can see that naïve literalism and biblical inerrancy come as a natural consequence. If you interpret the Bible metaphorically, what does that do to the dates that you're basing your calculations on? You don't have hard and fast numbers anymore. So the millenarian movements and innovations of 19th-century America are the crucial background to Fundamentalist notions of theology.

But Fundamentalism, as it emerged in the early 20th century, was at least as much a social as a religious movement and, once again, a reactionary one. The key stimulus was here social anxiety, anxiety particularly over social exclusion, mostly through the loss of a supposed old order—and that's rhetoric that is still with us. In the early 20th century, the anxiety was fear over the loss of a religiously oriented, locally independent, Anglo-Saxon Protestant America. In other words, outsiders—however you define that—were gaining positions of social culture and political stature. The perceived foes were actually diverse, but in general were simply modernity and change of all sorts, in particular, the rise of urban and learned culture and industrialization. Remember, this is the time in America where a fundamental shift is going on from an agrarian economy, an agrarian society, a rural society, to an urbanized industrialized one. That was a very traumatic change.

Anxiety over immigration was also key. Moreover, there was a sense of exclusion arising from more advanced methods of biblical exegesis, which the less educated couldn't follow and led to confusion. This constellation of sociopolitical anxieties of the early 20th century is the background not only to Fundamentalism, but also to the second Ku Klux Klan, which was organized in 1915 just as *The Fundamentals* were being published. Now I am not saying that the two were composed of the same people, but only that the two movements spring from similar historical and social circumstances, a sense of social displacement. People who suddenly realized that, after all, they didn't have a privileged place in an increasingly pluralistic America. Things were changing.

As an inherently reactionary movement, Fundamentalism thus developed around the core of negativity, an identity defined by opposition to things perceived as "other." This led increasingly towards belligerency. As one of the foremost historians of Fundamentalism in America writes, "A Fundamentalist is an Evangelical who is angry about something." What Fundamentalists have been angry about has changed frequently over time. In "The Fundamentals," it was largely higher criticism, while evolution in fact was treated quite benignly.

The explosion of belligerency against evolution in particular dates from World War I. World War I was a shock that we have difficulty today imagining; as the first really technological war it exposed barbarism in ways no one had imagined. World War I suggested that something had gone fundamentally wrong with Western culture. The confidence in progress and the promises of enlightenment that formed optimistic Victorian social and political rhetoric were blown to smithereens. Technology, the pride of Victorian civilization, was now used to make instruments of death. What went wrong?

For some, it was a decline in Traditionalist thinking, and it was not lost on some that Germany had been home to higher criticism and materialism. Others argued that the Germans had actually used Social Darwinism—the survival of the fittest in society—to justify aggression, while biological Darwinism, with its doctrine of common ancestry, reduced human beings to the status of animals.

There's another key point, though: the rise of public secondary school education. The period 1900 to 1920 witnessed an unprecedented growth in high schools. In 1890, there were about 200,000 high school students in America. By 1920, the number had surged to two million, a tenfold increase, and that would double again in the following decade. Thus, America's rural populations—which we have to remember at this time were incredibly isolated and had been since the founding of the frontiers—were suddenly exposed to modern thought and science for virtually the first time.

Another example could be read as another example of outsiders, in this case, the textbooks of predominantly northeast intelligentsia invading rural America. What's the easiest countermeasure? Ban the teaching of evolution in the schools. Thus, beginning in 1921 in Kentucky, laws were introduced in various state legislatures to do just that. Such a law, the Butler Act, was passed in Tennessee in 1925 and gave rise to the "Scopes Monkey Trial."

This trial has been dramatized on the stage and in film as the drama *Inherit the Wind* and has entered the American consciousness. In fact, what we have to realize is that the whole trial was a set-up. Once the Butler Act was passed, the American Civil Liberties Union looked for a test case to challenge the law, and several Tennessee communities actually vied for the case. But it was awarded eventually to Dayton, Tennessee, a town on the eastern edge of the state.

The town leaders of Dayton asked a local teacher, the 24-year old John T. Scopes, if he'd be willing to stand as a defendant. He was a perfect defendant. He was young and easy-going, and in fact he had only stood in as a substitute teacher for biology classes; it wasn't even his subject. And in those classes, he might or might not have ever mentioned evolution. He was no crusader for free speech and science, and neither were the town leaders. Their hope was to bring some free publicity to an economically struggling town.

The grand designs of the locals overwhelmed the modest test case that the ACLU had wanted. When the trial convened in July 1925, it was at least as much circus as it was trial. In fact, the whole court proceedings had to be moved out of the courthouse because, owing to the weight of all the spectators, the floor of the courtroom showed signs of collapse, so they set up outside on the lawn.

The problem was that big-guns, completely unwanted by the ACLU, showed up for the legal team. On the prosecution came William Jennings Bryan, former presidential candidate, famed orator, and now the Fundamentalist's main rallyer and loudest spokesman. One other thing about him: many of you may know that *The Wizard of Oz* is in part a political allegory. William Jennings Bryan is the cowardly lion.

Bryan bears much of the credit—or blame, depending on how you look at it—for turning the Fundamentalist movement towards evolution. For his defense, John Scopes chose America's most famous—some would say infamous—trial lawyer, Clarence Darrow. Bryan had begun crusading against evolution in 1922. He was convinced that evolution did lie at the heart of the deterioration of morality and civilization. He saw World War I in just these terms. As a perennial stumper and presidential candidate, he had embraced a simplistic populist creed. "The people," he said, "should have what they want." Now he extended this populism, his adulation of the average man—he himself was called "the Great Commoner"—into an aggressively anti-intellectual attack on science.

He referred in outraged tones to what he called an "oligarchy of scientists," telling Americans—regular Americans—what to believe. He seemed literally to believe that scientific questions could be settled by a majority vote, even if the majority didn't understand the questions. Bryan's militancy and belligerency on this issue—features that in fact frightened and shocked even his own wife—played well with rank-and-file Fundamentalists who eventually emulated the style.

No one will ever accuse Bryan of being an intellectual, nor will he ever escape the accusations of demagoguery that typified his public career. However, it would be wrong to think that his late-in-life crusade against evolution was nothing but bluster and foolishness. Instead, at the core, it reflected his traditional crusadings for workers' rights and human dignity, both of which he felt were imperiled by evolution. So really we can find fault with the way he went about it, but in fact his heart was probably, in one sense, in the right place.

The Scopes trial did not last long—one week in July 1925. Darrow and Bryan tried to turn it into a debate over Fundamentalism and evolution and nearly succeeded. But the judge tried, with greater success, to restrict the case to whether or not Scopes broke the Butler Act. Accordingly, there was no scientific or theological testimony allowed. The battle between Fundamentalism and modernity took place predominantly in the opposing statements of Darrow and Bryan and in a dramatic turn when Darrow put Bryan on the witness stand. The prosecution tried to prevent him from getting on the stand, but Bryan could never turn down a public forum.

As H.L. Mencken, who covered the trial for the *Baltimore Sun*, wrote, "It is a tragedy indeed to begin life as a hero and end it as a buffoon." And Bryan ended just that way. Darrow's questioning revealed that even Bryan himself could not adhere to naïve literalism and probably for the first time in his life, Bryan was forced to make his boisterous public statements seem self-consistent. He jabbered and blustered and tried to crack jokes, but cross-examination proved a very different environment from his usual bully pulpit and one to which he was singularly ill-suited.

Where was John Scopes? He never took the stand. But in the end, he was convicted and fined one hundred dollars. And that was all the ACLU really wanted, the beginning of an appeals process. But their hopes were dashed because Scopes's conviction was overturned at the first appeal on a technicality. As it turned out, Tennessee law forbade a judge to impose a fine of more than fifty dollars. And here in this case, the fine was a hundred.

After all the sound and fury, what did it accomplish? Not much directly. The Butler Act still stood. Given the wide press in print, in newsreel, and for the first time, the new technology of radio, Bryan's rantings only forced the sides further apart, and his death a week later left the Fundamentalists without a political leader. These factors, together with a new threat, that is, to defeat the presidential bid of Al Smith in 1928—God forbid, a New Yorker and a Catholic—made evolution slip from center position on their agenda. But after 1925, evolution also receded from biology textbooks, owing to publishers' concerns over the sales in Southern states.

The attempt to ban the teaching of evolution was not over, only held at bay by more pressing issues. A new spur came in the 1960s in the same form as it did in the teens—improved secondary school education. The trigger was Sputnik, launched in 1957. The initial lead of the Soviet Union in the emergent space race forced the American government to take a hard look at American education.

One result was a study of American high school curricula. What the studies found was appalling—massively outdated textbooks and much of the country with substandard instruction. This was no way to compete with the Russkies. The biology group, or BSCS for Biological Sciences Curriculum Study, produced massively improved biology texts for high schools in 1963. Mid-century American biology texts were little more than zoological and botanical compendia after the fashion of 19th-century books, but the new books used evolution as an organizing, explanatory principle, as professional biologists and college-level texts had been doing for decades. These new books were widely adopted.

But in a few years, the improved curriculum set off new attempts to ban evolution. Four states—Arkansas, Tennessee, Louisiana and

Mississippi—still had the 1920s-era laws on the books. A challenge was made in Arkansas in 1965 by the Arkansas Educational Association charging the law to be unconstitutional on the grounds of infringement of free speech by schoolteachers. It took them just two hours to convince a judge to strike down the law. But it also took the Arkansas Supreme Court just two sentences to reinstate it. It then went to the Federal Supreme Court, and in 1968, the justices ruled the antievolution law unconstitutional because, "It selects from a body of knowledge a particular segment, which it proscribed for the sole reason that it is deemed to conflict with a particular religious doctrine." So, finally, 1968, the 1925 Butler Act is struck down with other similar statutes.

With the banning of evolution precluded, antievolutionists turned to a new strategy: the "equal-time" strategy, that is, if you are going to teach evolution, then you have to give equal time to—well, what? Something had to be found as an alternative, and this is the origin of "creation science." The roots of creation science lie earlier than 1968, but it was the Supreme Court decision of that year that consolidated it into a legally promotable evolution alternative. What is it? Where did it come from?

Before we answer that question, we need to take a close look at the labels "creationism" and "creationist." Labels like product names are important and often for some of the same reasons. Antievolution sounds negative. It's that annoying "anti" at the beginning. So antievolutionists took to the more upbeat name "creationists." But the two words are not interchangeable. If they were, one would have to be either a creationist or an evolutionist. But this is a false dichotomy. Most Christians are in fact both. Be on the lookout for these false dichotomies in antievolutionist rhetoric. They are very common.

Creationism encompasses a wide range of viewpoints. Let's analyze it. The first division within creationists is between general and special creationists. General creationists affirm only in a nonspecific way that God is the ultimate creator. They make no claims about what it is exactly He did or does. Special creationists, on the other hand, assign Him one or more specific "special" roles in creation. Special creationists are themselves divided into two parts: progressive and strict. Progressive creationists interpret the six days of Genesis allegorically, while strict ones do it literally. Still not the end of the taxonomy.

Progressive creationists, that is, the allegorical interpreters, are further divided in two. The first view God's actions as single or very few, for example, initiating life or infusing the human soul. After an initial creative act *ex nihilo*—that's enough to make you a creationist right there—natural forces within creation accomplished everything, say, for one or two special interventions. This, for example, is a position of the Catholic Church.

The other group of progressive creationists require a large, perhaps an infinite number, of separate creative acts for each species or genus. The former group is closer to naturalism, the latter, closer to supernaturalism. But wait, there is more. The strict creationists, that is, the biblical literalists, are also divided in two. One group adheres to the Gap theory; that is, they envision a long epoch between the initial creation in the six days. The other are the young earth creationists who, along with rejecting evolution, entirely reject geological time and consider the earth less than 10,000 years old. So in speaking of creationists, we have to identify which flavor we are really talking about.

With that taxonomy in place, let's get back to creation science. Creation science represents strict creationists, biblical literalist views, and generally of the young earth variety. While it originated in the 1960s, its roots are older and based in what's called "flood geology." We've seen flood geology before—the notion that Noah's Flood was a global geological event explaining fossils, mountains, canyons, strata. We saw its emergence in the 17th century—the late 17th century—its revival by Mosaic geologists in the early 19th century, but by 1900, it was essentially dead.

But you know, some bad ideas are like Dracula; just when you think they are dead and buried, all of a sudden, you feel their breath on your neck again. Flood geology and Manichaeanism that we've talked about are two examples. Flood geology rose from its coffin in 1923, not merely coincidentally at the height of the Fundamentalist antievolution furor. The one who pulled the stake out this time was George McCready Price in his book entitled *The New Geology*. Now Price was a Seventh-day Adventist and so his source is clear.

Do you remember the Millerites, the pre-millennialists who awaited apocalypse in 1844? What did they do in 1845? Well, some of them redid the calculations, and others became the Seventh-day Adventists, following the teenaged prophetess named Ellen White.

White, as a result of a vision, asserted that Noah's Flood was the central event in geology. Of course, she didn't actually need an interview with the Almighty to come to this conclusion, just picking up any of the various popular Mosaic geology texts would have done just as well.

Price obviously drew upon White as a source. But his 1923 claims didn't have much immediate impact. The impact came only at the start of the second antievolution furor when the views were revived. In 1961, there appeared *The Genesis Flood*, a book by Henry M. Morris and John C. Whitcomb. This book and these authors gave rise to creation science and to the founding of the Creation Science Society in 1963.

Legal arguments for equal time for creation science had some initial success, notably in Arkansas and Louisiana. Such arguments, like those for teaching intelligent design, at first glance, appeal to American ideals of fairness. Such measures were, however, turned back in 1987 when the Supreme Court recognized creation science as a religious doctrine and not science.

In fact, it's a very specific doctrine, not to be confused with orthodox Christian doctrine. It's a minority view, that of young earth creationists, one of the groups down on the corner of our taxonomy of creationists. In fact, in the legal case in 1981, virtually every mainstream Christian denomination—Catholic and Protestant—lined up to support striking down the equal-time law. In response to this external pressure, antievolution continued to evolve.

The next variations masked any identifiably religious content in order to pass constitutional muster. Remember, this is not an intellectual movement; it's a legal and a political one now. The goal remains steady, but various pathways are closed off by the courts, and new ones have to be found. It doesn't necessarily require new ideas, just new strategies. The mutated offspring was neocreationism. This next generation appeared first in the form of abrupt appearance theory, simply that new life forms abruptly appeared—basically creation without mentioning God. This weak variation was not fitted to long-term survival and became extinct very soon. A more successful adaptation is intelligent design, which we examined in an earlier lecture, and it continues to proliferate and develop at present.

As we can see from this lecture, the antievolution stance developed in the United States in Fundamentalist circles since the 1920s has focused primarily on keeping evolution out of secondary school teaching or to distract from evolution by presenting some alternative, more alignable with strict biblical literalist perspectives.

There is a continued success here in a way, since, as occurred in the late 1920s, textbook publishers have tended to decrease the coverage of evolution in order to avoid upsetting their profits, which is what their business is all about. Likewise, public school boards, principals and some teachers find that the path of least resistance is simply to avoid or give short shrift to evolution. One result is that, in the U.S., the greatest coverage of evolution in high school biology now takes place in Catholic schools and in other private schools that weren't set up by Fundamentalists themselves.

I couldn't end this lecture without pointing out how this evolution controversy of 20th-century America, more than the 19th-century English issue, instantiates in many ways the conflict thesis for science-religion interactions, although we should be clear not to neglect the political and social dimensions, which are just as important.

In our next and final lecture, we will consider how these current developments distort our historical perspective. We will also try to draw together some issues we've treated in this course and suggest a way to reposition and reduce this conflict.

Lecture Twelve
Past, Present, and Future

Scope:

In this concluding lecture, we survey what we have seen and learned in this course and endeavor to place our own times in historical context. Notably, we conclude that no single blanket description is satisfactory for describing the complexity of science/religion interactions in Christianity over time. The productive engagements between science and theology should be duly stressed. Much of the current-day clashes occur between extremists—religious and scientistic fundamentalists. This lecture proposes that the historical perspective is the best way to transcend and defuse such clashes. The extremist groups ignore historical background (theological and scientific) in favor of self-promoting mythologies, trivialize or fail to understand complex philosophical issues worked out in the past, and are not representative of the totality of science or of Christianity. Historical sense allows us to lift the potentially valuable discourse about and between science and religion to higher, more intellectual, and productive levels.

Outline

I. The interactions between science and religion have been complex over time and are not reducible to simple blanket descriptions.

    A. The warfare thesis depends on the existence of separate "camps" of theologians and scientists; this is a relatively recent division.

    B. The movement of ideas back and forth between theological and scientific thought has been more usual.

        1. Scientific and theological thought have grown up together in Western thought and share several methods and aspirations.

        2. Christian theology developed certain methods, perspectives, and cultural environments key to modern scientific inquiry.

        3. The Christian Church has provided important institutional support (patronage) for studies of the natural world.

4. Likewise, science has provided theology with a truer sense of man's place in the natural world.
5. Christian theology has proven itself remarkably flexible in its ability to adopt, adapt, and explore new scientific findings.

II. Although clearly false as a historical model, the warfare thesis seems supported by current events, particularly involving evolution.

A. A historical perspective provides a clearer view of the real status of the current debates and points out particular features of interest.

B. Science and theology have experienced nearly opposite trajectories in terms of professionalization, authority, and status.
1. Scientific activity has been regularized by professionalization, granting it greater authority.
2. Theological activity has become diffused by decreased ability to professionalize theologians; the result has been lower-level theology and a loss of status and authority.
3. This trend in theology is exemplified by the triviality of the theological content of the anti-evolution debate (biblical literalism) relative to historical theological issues.

C. Historical study holds the promise to correct this problem by indicating the diversity and complexity of past theological debates and responses.
1. Traditional Christian theology shows biblical literalism to be a non-issue.
2. Consider, for example, the case of B. B. Warfield (1851–1921), the strong defender of biblical inerrancy who also supported evolution.
3. The historical background, once known, forces people to ask what makes biblical literalism/evolution an issue now.
4. One cause may simply be unfamiliarity with historical theology and current "high-end" (that is, philosophically sophisticated) theology.
5. Thus, the study of history is again a solution.

III. Rather than merely exemplifying the warfare thesis, both parties involved in the current controversy have adopted it as a model for their own behavior.

   A. A warfare metaphor appeals to the Manichean mindset of many fundamentalists.

   B. Some scientists, crusading for materialism and atheism, support fundamentalist fears.

      1. Such scientists have often forgotten the difference between a *professional policy* of not invoking supernatural action and a *personal credo* against everything supernatural.

      2. Historical perspective (again) reminds us of the difference.

      3. Scientists should avoid making theological or metaphysical claims when they are unqualified to do so.

      4. An example is the assertion that the inherent randomness of mutation and contingency of natural selection excludes the possibility of divine guidance of evolution. This position is refuted by the 2002 statement "Communion and Stewardship" by the International Theological Commission.

   C. The loudest combatants in the evolution controversy are both extremists.

      1. Their arguments tend to harden positions and create division where it need not exist.

      2. The perception of the controversy ignores the vast field of cooperation and intelligent conversation by the majority in between.

      3. Fundamentalists do not have the right to speak for Christianity; declamatory supporters of scientism do not have the right to speak for science.

   D. What both lack is a sense of humility before the complexity of the world and man's place in it.

Essential Reading:

International Theological Commission, "Communion and Stewardship," chapter 3, esp. sections 61–80.

Supplementary Reading:

Brooke, *Science and Religion*, Postscript (pp. 321–347).

Questions to Consider:

1. At several points in this course, the issue of authority has emerged, either explicitly or implicitly. (For example, who speaks for science? Who speaks for theology? How does one decide between rival scientific interpretations or between rival theological perspectives?) Think about how authority is gained and how it is respected (or not) in an ideal world and in the real world. How does one achieve the ability to speak authoritatively about scientific issues? About theological issues? Do the answers to the previous two questions differ? Should they?

2. There are certain basic beliefs and practices that are integral to Christianity (that is, without these beliefs and practices, the religion would not be Christian), for example, the statements of the Nicene Creed. Are there analogous basic beliefs and practices for science? What are they? What would be the consequences of abandoning them?

Note: I ended the final lecture with the Latin phrase *Ite missa est*, meaning literally, "go, it is sent." These words are borrowed from the last line of the Latin Tridentine Mass (in fact, the term *Mass* is derived from this concluding line). My intent was not only to arrest your attention and curiosity but also to draw upon the rich associations and multiple meanings of the phrase (in a non-sacrilegious way, I trust) to imply that although I have sent you some thoughts and now the course is ended, the issues covered pass far beyond the short duration of these lectures. Thus, I intend the line to be taken as gentle encouragement to continue your study and consideration of science and religion issues as encountered in everyday life.

Lecture Twelve—Transcript
Past, Present, and Future

Now we've arrived at our 12th and final lecture. We've covered a great deal of material in terms of both time period and subject matter, and now is the time for us to review a little bit of this and see where we've come to. One thing that should be clear at this point is how complex, how diverse, the interactions between science and theology have been over time. We cannot apply simple blanket descriptions to them, and I hope I have convinced you that we shouldn't want to either. We would then lose the engaging complexity, the intricacies of the issues, and the profound ideas that we've encountered.

Certainly, the old "warfare thesis" can no longer stand. Its starting assumption, that there existed, in the past, two well-defined and warring camps, one under the standard of science, the other under the standard of theology or religion, is simply mistaken. We've seen many thinkers whose work freely traversed what today we would consider as the boundaries or the borders between science and theology. Have there been conflicts between a given scientific statement and a given theological one? Of course there have. But there have also been conflicts between two theological positions or between two scientific positions. Conflict can be an opportunity for discussion, exploration, and discovery, or an opportunity for becoming shrill and self-righteous and sulking off to our respective corners. That's a free choice. But it's also clear which is the intelligent and the productive choice.

What we've seen in the foregoing lectures is often, though not exclusively, the movement and development of ideas and concepts and methods back and forth between natural and theological inquiry. This really shouldn't surprise us because science and theology, after all, share a great deal in common. They are both human strivings for knowledge, operating by the cooperative exercise of faith and reason. They are both activities of human beings and both expressions of human desires, most of all our fundamental human desire to know.

Theological and scientific inquiry in the West grew up together, often interacting, often sharing methods and goals, sometimes encouraging and sometimes chiding one another. On the one side, theology developed some of the methods and approaches that modern science takes for granted, and often, by the way I should say, imagines sometimes being its own creation. The disputational nature of scholastic theology developed basic rules and methods of logical argumentation and probably more importantly instilled irremovably in Western culture a culture of disputation.

Try to imagine good science without dispute. It's hard to imagine as good theology without dispute. One specific appropriation from theology to modern science that we've mentioned is the preference for naturalism in giving explanations. This is a key methodological principle for modern science, but its foundations lie with the profound thoughts of medieval theologians who realized that only natural causation, that is, secondary causation, is really comprehensible to the human mind. Therefore, only secondary causation has any explanatory power.

One thing we haven't mentioned explicitly in this course is the vast institutional patronage that natural philosophical inquiry obtained from ecclesiastical sources, from cathedral schools to the first universities, to great churches doubling as observatories, and the enumerable scholars whose work in natural philosophy was facilitated by the support of their being in Holy Orders.

In our lectures, we've mentioned just a few of them, including St. Albert the Great, Roger Bacon, Copernicus, Casendi, Mersenne, Castelli, Ray, and Lemaître. There are, of course, many others. For its part, scientific study has made its own contributions to theology. Perhaps one of the most notable ways is in terms of new perspectives on the world, in other words, a truer sense of man's place in time, space, and nature. Without a doubt, some of these new revelations were received with discomfort or resistance. But real theology, no less than science, is about the search for truth. It is not, as some people now erroneously enough wave it off, just about opinion. Theology has come away from the encounter with new views of man's place in relation to the creator of time, space, and nature.

I remind you also of St. Augustine's comments on the need for up-to-date demonstrated natural knowledge among theologians and exegetes. And as we've seen throughout the course, Christian theology has proven itself remarkably flexible in its ability to adopt, adapt, and explore new scientific findings—to see in essence what they mean.

Even though the warfare model is wrong-headed as a historical description, some current events do seem to lend to it an air of credibility. The violent fulminations, declamations, and legal wrangling that have taken place between antievolutionist Fundamentalists and the scientific establishment or the educational establishment since the 1920s seems to instantiate a model of warring adversaries. And since this issue is closest to us in time and space, it naturally looms the largest. And so it tempts us to read the conflict back in time. And here is where historical perspective is so necessary.

What does it do? It gives us a high vantage point from which to survey the scene. By taking us above the current fray, it helps us distinguish between local and general phenomena and helps to see larger trends and directions. Even better, it gives us a host of reckoning points by which to measure our own times. What does the perspective of history have to say about the current tussle? Well, the historical issue of professionalization explains a striking feature of the antievolution conflict. Professionalization imposes standards of education and training on those entering the field. Their reward is recognized authority.

In the Middle Ages and early modern period, a person interested in the study of the natural world simply acted on his interests, provided he had the leisure to do so. For example, in the 17th century, how did Steno start looking at rocks and fossils? He just started picking them up, collecting them, and studying them. Robert Boyle had no formal education after age 12. Study of the natural world, natural philosophy, was in this sense an amateur activity. Since that time, however, professionalization has raised the bar for entry. It's heightened the social recognition and thus the authority that scientists enjoy.

Look at the other side; theology was highly professionalized in the Middle Ages. A doctorate in theology required at least 10 years of advanced study, much more than was needed for, say, lawyers and physicians. The criteria for entrance to the Guild of Theology were stringent and well defined. Those without the degree could neither teach nor practice theology. Authority for those admitted was thus assured.

But following the reformation and the rise of personal interpretations, the restriction of theologizing to a professional class began to erode. With the proliferation of countless minor religious sects in frontier America, it became impossible to monitor. Today, while there are still many professional theologians with extensive training, there are also many others, more, who write or speak on theological topics with little or no training.

Moreover, because high-end theology—by high-end theology, I mean philosophically and intellectually sophisticated—is every bit as complicated as any other high level intellectual field, it is almost entirely the low-end material, of which there is more out there, that finds popular exposure and currency. In other words, it fills entirely the theological niche in popular conceptions.

This trend, along with other considerations, has resulted in a loss of authority, not just for theologians, but for theology itself. Indeed, today even many well-read people are unaware of the continuing tradition of sophisticated professional theology. Thus, science and theology have followed opposite trajectories, science becoming all the time more and more professional, more and more advanced in the public eye, theology, less and less.

The point I want to make is that the trend for theology manifests itself in the inherent caliber of the theological issues involved in the current evolution-antievolution debate. From earlier episodes, we sampled challenging issues about the limits and powers of human knowledge—the difficulty of identifying causation reliably and the means by which God can act in the world. All of these are knotty subjects of long-term discussion and interest to generations of theologians. Generations of theologians applied their reasoning to these problems. And though I mentioned at one point, this was the case not just in Christianity, but as well in Islam and Judaism, often in similar terms.

But the current conflict stemming from Fundamentalism concerns no intellectual issue more complicated than whether Genesis I is to be read literally or not. Intellectually speaking, it is very hard not to find this astonishingly trivial and uninteresting in comparison to earlier issues. Given the publicity surrounding these current events, it's easy to see why so many people today are surprised to learn of the existence and continuing development and practice of sophisticated rational theology—high-end theology. And if Fundamentalist statements on evolution remain all the theology that the general public is exposed to, then the status of and respect for theology will continue to decline.

Well, the perspective of history not only points this out, but offers a solution. There is an old hymn that was, at least at one time, popular in Fundamentalist circles. And if you've ever seen the movie *Inherit the Wind*, based on the Scopes Trial, you will remember the scenes of crowds singing it in the streets, "Give me that old-time religion." I think I'm justified in taking old-time religion to mean historical religion. So what does historical religion have to say about the current issue of evolution and biblical literalism? Well, basically it tells us it's a non-issue. Rare are the instances of naïve literalism being used as a bludgeon for natural philosophical scientific ideas.

Galileo certainly had some problems on a related score in the nervous aftermath of the Council of Trent, but even then, for every Dominican who saw a problem with heliocentrism in Joshua's story, there was a cardinal who claimed that the Bible was to tell us how to go to heaven, not how the heavens go.

The Middle Ages accepted St. Augustine's recommendations on biblical interpretation. St. Augustine's 15 years of careful thought and rational analysis to create a literal commentary on Genesis I concluded with the idea of an instantaneous moment of creation that produced a universe that developed over time into the form we see. And no medieval theologian would have raised an eyebrow at the idea that living beings could arise spontaneously, naturally, out of nonliving matter. That's old-time religion.

But if something a little less old is desired—and the subtext here might be a little less Catholic perhaps—then current biblical inerrantists can reach back to their own immediate history. There's an important history there, too. Consult, for example, with the late-19th-century's strongest champion of biblical inerrancy, Benjamin Breckenridge Warfield, a conservative theologian at Princeton Theological Seminary. Against higher criticism, Warfield defended the position that the whole Bible is a divine revelation free from error. His doctrine of biblical inerrancy is the basis for current-day strict creationism and a mainstay of Fundamentalist belief. Yet the historical fact is that Warfield was not only open to the theory of evolution, on occasion, he openly advocated it. There is some more old-time religion.

The recognition of these historically held positions demands an answer to one particular question: If so many devout and highly learned Christians over time rejected naïve biblical literalism and had no problem even with the idea of the spontaneous origin of life, and even the prime architect of modern biblical inerrancy was willing to accept evolution, what's the problem now?

Some would suggest that the problem is to be sought as much in a concern for political and social control as with any theological position. But for many people—and I think especially young people—much of the problem may simply be an unfamiliarity with good sources. They are bombarded with so much bad—no, pseudo-theology—that they have never witnessed the real thing. In that case, the solution is easy: the study of history.

One hopeful sign I have seen of late are a few publications by Evangelicals that present historical materials and use them to educate, for example, young earth creationists that the literal six days of creation is not the old-time traditional view and why. Now some might respond that the writings and interpretations of earlier theologians are not relevant to them today. But that seems to me rather like a physicist saying that the laws discovered by Newton, Laplace, and Maxwell are no longer relevant to him.

And of course being realistic, I acknowledge that there will be some who refuse to engage in any discussion whatsoever. They will say, "Well, it just is that way" or "I believe what I believe;" there is fideism again. In which case, I find that I can save my limited strength for people who want to discuss things rather than flying to an anti-intellectual state that precludes it. Not all will be saved.

But the perspective of history provides a further observation, namely, rather than merely exemplifying the warfare thesis, both parties involved in the current controversy seem to have actually adopted it as a model for behavior. The fiery rhetoric of William Jennings Bryan that ignited opposition to Darwinism was a formative pattern for Fundamentalists. And perhaps at a deeper level, it seems that the warfare model appeals to Fundamentalists' inherently Manichean mindset—good and evil, light and dark, us and them. But if some—and I emphasize the word "some"—Fundamentalists are guilty of fanning the flames of war, then so are some scientists, and to an equal extent. There are those in the scientific community who make a point of evangelizing for materialism and atheism.

We heard a few lectures ago Haeckel's dogmatic and pompous creed about the cell annulling the deity. I mentioned also previously that some Fundamentalists' depiction of the scientific establishment as aggressively and inherently atheistic is an example of the error of collectivism. But in reading the Haeckels, the Hoyles, the Sagans, the Dawkins, the Drapers, and their tribe, one can see easily the foundations of this depiction and why it causes justifiable anxiety.

There are today notable and high-profile scientists who use op-ed pieces, popular books, and programs, and other public pulpits to proclaim the gospels of materialism, atheism, and scientism. When such positions are argued for rationally and with philosophical sophistication, it will certainly lead to interesting and productive discussion. But too often the claims are philosophically naïve and clothed in arrogant sarcasm and dismissive disdain. That's no way to carry out a discussion.

Similarly, much media reporting on scientific developments either uncritically recapitulates unreasonable scientistic boasts or, by simplifying the issues, fall inadvertently into philosophically naïve claims that impinge on other fields, including theology, or that raise legitimate concerns among those seriously concerned with the issues. If, as I mentioned before, some Fundamentalists misunderstand the difference between methodological naturalism and philosophical naturalism, it's in part because some vocal scientists do so as well. Or maybe the scientists have forgotten the difference. And here again, history comes to the rescue. History is often about reminding us of things that we've forgotten.

Part of the process of scientific professionalization was the creation of boundaries of what was and was not the domain of scientists. We saw, for example, the early geologists who just wanted to mind their rocks without being drawn into larger agendas. As natural philosophy was being paired down and divvied up into the various sciences, pronouncements on ultimate origins, purposes, and meanings were excluded from new scientific discourse. The days in which a Newton could talk about the being and attribute of God in a physics text were over.

The commitment to naturalistic explanations became explicit. The rules of appropriate scientific conduct, as we can call them, had both philosophical and pragmatic origins. On the one hand, certain topics were seen as simply lying outside the boundaries that were being drawn for science. On the other, the avoidance of such topics was a way to avoid being drawn into discussions and debates outside the new boundaries of science.

I think the crucial point here is that these points were instituted as rules of the game, not creeds. Some scientists seem to have forgotten the difference. Participating in scientific discourse means you are not allowed to use, for example, supernatural intervention as causation, or to stand in for explanation. "Then a miracle occurs" is not scientific. It's not an allowed move on the chessboard of science, if you will. In such cases, the only allowed move is to suspend judgment and say that science offers no explanation. But science does not tell you—in fact, cannot tell you—that no supernatural activity exists or that God might not be operating behind secondary causation. A scientist is perfectly free, of course, to adopt an atheistic or materialist stance, but not to say that this position is a necessary consequence of science.

There is a fundamental difference between allowed professional behavior and personal belief. And if some scientists, rightly enough, object to the intrusion of the un-credentialed into their field of play, then as a matter of professional courtesy, if nothing else, they have to mind their own manners when they try to play on the equally professionalized field of high-end theology.

In the specific case of evolution, an argument made by some scientists is that the random nature of mutation and the contingent nature of natural selection rules out any possibility of divine guidance. This position is addressed in one of those high-end theological documents the general public rarely gets to see. I couldn't resist one last chance of sharing one of these sort of documents with you. It's a document from the International Theological Commission entitled *Communion and Stewardship* and was published in 2002 and approved by the man now called Benedict XVI. As part of a lengthy argument about the Christians' duty towards environmentalism, it outlines human beings' place in the created world. It reaffirms, for example, John Paul's 1996 comments about evolution and then goes on to explain that neo-Darwinians who rule out any divine role in evolution display, "a misunderstanding of the nature of divine causality."

Are you ready for one last go at divine causality? Here it is—it's a little bit lengthy, but I will try to parse it for you.

Many neo-Darwinian scientists have concluded that if evolution is a radically contingent materialistic process, driven by natural selection and random genetic variation, then there can be no place in it for divine providential causality. But true contingency in the created order is not incompatible with a purposeful divine providence. Thus, even the outcome of a truly contingent natural process can, nonetheless, fall within God's providential plan for creation. Any evolutionary mechanism that is contingent can only be contingent because God made it so. An unguided evolutionary process, one that falls outside the bounds of divine providence, simply cannot exist because [quoting St. Thomas] 'The causality of God who is the first agent extends to all being. It necessarily follows that all things inasmuch as they participate in existence must likewise be subject to divine providence.'

There you have it, high-end theology.

In other words, God made all the secondary causes. Therefore, any effects they produce, even if contingent or random, are ultimately linked to God's creative act. Thus the document concludes that, "neo-Darwinians who adduce random genetic variation and natural selection as evidence that the process of evolution is absolutely unguided are straying beyond what can be demonstrated by science." In other words, there's a limit to human knowledge. We really can't determine where chains of causation come to an end.

I come to the ironic conclusion then that strong antievolutionists and strong partisans of scientism have a great deal in common. They are both Fundamentalists. The battle is going on between two groups of extremists—two minorities within the respective groups. They have every right in the world to engage in this battle if they like, but there is a consequence of the way in which it is being carried out. There's simply a lot of fallout, a lot of civilian injuries, if you will, for the majority over whose head they are firing their missiles. What I mean is that extremist positions have the effect of alienating moderates and deepening divisions. Loud declarations from either end tend to overwhelm more moderate voices either by greater volume or, more likely, by greater coverage in the media. Extremist views tend to be simpler, less nuanced, and thus easier to communicate in a 15-second sound byte or newspaper column. Try to imagine, for example, *USA Today* trying to report on this commission document I just quoted from.

This leaves the general public with the impression of a radical, irreconcilable division between science generally and religion generally, a conclusion that the historical record and current reality oppose. In fact, such a division seems to be in fact what extremists want—a life or death struggle for preeminence. Sort of Darwinian, isn't it? On the one side, we find one ID supporter claiming that legal challenges to teaching evolution are about, "Who is going to sit at the head of the table?"; on the other, the baseless and empirically false assertion that it's impossible to be both a scientist and a theist. For those in the middle, the best recourse is again—guess what—history. To the historical perspective.

This course has illustrated a wide diversity of interactions and pointed out areas of commonality between scientific and theological methods and aims. Most clearly of all, I hope, is that it has shown how things have not always been as they are now, nor need they be. It emphasizes how current struggles are or are not local and limited and how they hide from our view the intricacy of the real intellectual issues. Now of course, Fundamentalists are welcome to vent their position, but it should also be perfectly clear that Fundamentalists do not have the right to speak for Christianity as a whole. They are not representative. From the perspective of the here and now, they are a minority and, from the perspective of the whole history of Christianity, considerably less than that.

More importantly, they have little claim to authority when compared to historical theological positions or present-day high-end theology. They like to use the unmodified name of Christian in referring to themselves, but this is in fact, if we analyze it, a usurping presumption. In exactly the same way, the vociferous advocates of a materialistic scientism do not have the right to speak for science, scientists, and the scientific establishment.

What seems to be in the shortest supply on both sides is a sense of humility before the complexity of the world and the difficult issues surrounding man's place in it. Conflicts? No. Disagreements will invariably arise between people working in different fields or in the same field. These are the results of the tentative, often provisional, nature of our understanding, an effect of fallible human beings groping towards knowledge.

We've come now to the end of our course. We've surveyed some of the high points of the interactions of science and religion and ignored an embarrassingly large amount. Obviously, there are many more episodes to study, many more lessons to be learned; however, we have been able in our time together to identify some key issues and themes, to explore some of the interesting events. and to meet some of the interesting people.

My hope is that this will provide a starting point for you in your own further exploration and consideration of what will remain a developing subject. For now, I trust that this will be enough, *Ite missa est*.

[**Note**: I ended the final lecture with the Latin phrase *Ite missa est*, meaning literally, "go, it is sent." These words are borrowed from the last line of the Latin Tridentine Mass (in fact, the term *Mass* is derived from this concluding line). My intent was not only to arrest your attention and curiosity but also to draw upon the rich associations and multiple meanings of the phrase (in a non-sacrilegious way, I trust) to imply that although I have sent you some thoughts and now the course is ended, the issues covered pass far beyond the short duration of these lectures. Thus, I intend the line to be taken as gentle encouragement to continue your study and consideration of science and religion issues as encountered in everyday life.]

Timeline

313 ....Edict of Milan legalizes Christianity in the Roman Empire.

325 ....Ecumenical Council of Nicaea.

354–430.......................................Life of St. Augustine.

410 ....Rome sacked by Alaric.

476 ....Last of the (western) Roman emperors slain by the barbarian Odoacer.

800 ....Charlemagne crowned Holy Roman Emperor.

c. 1020...School of Chartres founded.

c. 1200...University of Paris established; Oxford, about 20 years later.

1205 ....St. Dominic founds the Order of Preachers (Dominicans).

1257 ....St. Thomas Aquinas begins teaching at Paris.

1277 ....Condemnation of 1277; 219 propositions condemned at the University of Paris.

1540 ....Society of Jesus (Jesuits) established.

1543 ....Copernicus's *De revolutionibus* published.

1545–1563...................................Council of Trent.

1610 ....Galileo's telescopic discoveries appear in the *Sidereus Nuncius*.

1616 ....Copernicus's book is "suspended until corrected"; Galileo told not to teach Copernicanism as true.

1618–1648 ....Thirty Years' War ravages central Europe.

1620 ....Plymouth colony established in Massachusetts.

1627 ....Robert Boyle born.

1632 ....Galileo's *Dialogues on the Two Chief World Systems* published; the next year, he is tried and abjures.

1642 ....Birth of Newton; death of Galileo.

1658 ....Gassendi's natural philosophical system published.

1660 ....Royal Society of London founded; given Royal Charter in 1662.

1669 ....Steno's work on fossils and strata published.

1692 ....Boyle Lectures commence.

1749 ....Buffon's first theories on the origin of the Earth appear.

1776 ....American Declaration of Independence.

1779 ....Eichhorn's *Urgeschichte* launches "higher criticism."

1796 ....Laplace's nebular hypothesis.

1802 ....Paley's *Natural Theology* published.

1807 ....Geological Society of London founded.

1830s ....*Bridgewater Treatises* published.

1831–1836 ....Darwin's trip around the world on HMS *Beagle*.

1844 ....Anonymous publication of *Vestiges of the Natural History of Creation*.

1844	In the United States, the world fails to end (again).
1859	Darwin's *Origin of Species* published.
1874	Hodge's *What Is Darwinism?* and Draper's *Conflict* published.
1896	White's final two-volume treatment of his warfare thesis published.
1910–1915	*The Fundamentals* printed and widely distributed.
1914–1918	World War I.
1925	Scopes' Monkey Trial.
1927	Lemaître proposes an expanding universe and a "primordial atom."
1968	Laws forbidding the teaching of evolution struck down by the U.S. Supreme Court.
1990s	The term *intelligent design* is coined; legal wranglings over the teaching of evolution in public schools continues in the United States.

Glossary

accommodation (doctrine of): An idea, proposed by St. Augustine and others in the patristic period and essentially universally accepted by mainstream orthodox Christianity, that biblical expressions were "accommodated" to the limited understanding and knowledge of the primitive people that made up their original audience.

ancilla: Latin for "handmaiden"; compare the English derivative *ancillary*. Used in the history of science to describe the status of the natural sciences relative to theology in the Middle Ages, as enunciated most influentially in the writings of St. Augustine and other patristics.

biblicism: A theological position holding that the Bible is the sole source of authority for Christianity. Accepted in varying degrees by Protestants; rejected by Catholics and Orthodox.

collectivism: In this context, a fallacy in historical methodology whereby the positions held by a single or small number of individuals are unwarrantably attached to a wider group to which they are considered to belong.

communis cursus naturae: Literally, "the common course of nature"; in other words, the routine, ordinary, and usual ways in which natural phenomena occur.

Council of Trent: A highly significant meeting of Catholic theologians and hierarchy that took place in the northern Italian city of Trento from 1545 to 1563. The purpose was to address the problem of Protestantism by internal reforms, regularization of doctrine, and measures to prevent further schism.

creatio ex nihilo: "Creation out of nothing," an article of Christian faith stressing that God alone is eternal and is the creator of everything.

creation science: A body of notions proposed, beginning in the 1980s, as an "alternative" to accepted scientific ideas regarding geological and cosmological history and, especially, biological evolution. Creation science bases itself on naïve literalist readings of Genesis 1 and flood geology.

creationism: Generally speaking, any view that posits a creation of the world by God. There are, however, enormously broad varieties of views that can fall under this rubric, ranging from Young-Earth creationism at one end (that is, the Earth is less than 10,000 years old and Genesis 1 is a literally true account of creation) to simply positing a single initial creative act (such as initiating the Big Bang).

criticism, higher and lower: Two views on how to interpret the Bible. Higher criticism, initiated in the 18th century, applies the standard textual tools, applicable to any historical text, to the Bible and asks questions about authorship, original context, influences, and so on. Lower criticism rejects such tools.

Day-Age theory: A position on the interpretation of Genesis 1 that holds that the "days" of creation refer to enormous epochs of time.

deism: A theistic position in which the deity is envisioned as impersonal, that is, a rejection of the Christian (or Jewish or Islamic) God.

design argument: An argument for the existence of God based on the belief that there is design in the visible world and, thus, a designer.

determinism: The idea that future events are pre-determined; there is no free will.

dualism: In the context of this course, the division of the world into contending good and evil forces; see **Manicheanism**.

epistemology: The study of knowledge; epistemology studies what we know (or can know) and how we know it (or think we know it).

fideism: An approach to religion that emphasizes faith at the expense of reason and, in its stronger expressions, holds that no part of the body of faith can be subjected to rational inspection or analysis; an inherently *anti-theological* position.

flood geology: The use of Noah's Flood as an explanation for geological phenomena (mountains, fossils, canyons, and so on). Although such ideas were suggested tentatively in the late 17th century, a distinct "flood geology" is the product of the 19th and 20th centuries and was an explicit reaction against scientific geological views of an ancient Earth.

Gap theory: A position on the interpretation of Genesis 1 that holds that although the "days" are actual 24-hour periods, an immense span of time can be inserted either before the six days or between certain days.

geocentric: Literally, "Earth-centered"; used to refer to the Aristotelian, Ptolemaic, and Tychonic systems, in which the Earth is at the center of the cosmos.

geokinetic: Literally, "Earth moving"; used to refer to cosmic systems in which the Earth is in motion, such as the Copernican system.

geostatic: Literally, "earth stationary"; used to refer to cosmic systems in which the earth is at rest.

God of the gaps: An unsatisfactory view of God generated when divine intervention is called upon to "fill in" gaps (generally temporary) in otherwise natural explanations of the natural world.

heliocentric: Literally, "Sun-centered"; used to refer to the Copernican system. (Actually, Copernicus's system has the Sun slightly off center and is more rigorously labeled heliostatic, that is, with a stationary Sun.)

hexameral treatises: A genre of theological writings of the patristic and medieval periods. Hexameral (derived from the Greek for "six days") treatises are commentaries on Genesis 1; as such, they were important loci for serious inquiries and theories about scientific subjects.

instrumentalism: A view that holds that our scientific theories and explanations are not (or need not) be literally true and are satisfactory as long as they "save the phenomena," that is, give a plausible and consistent explanation of what we see. Theories are instruments or tools, not final explanations. Compare **realism**.

literalism, naïve: A kind of biblical interpretation that holds that the "surface meaning" of the Bible is literally true. Naïve literalism, popular among fundamentalists and many evangelicals, is a fairly modern innovation—dating after the Protestant Reformation—and needs to be distinguished from more traditional literalism (such as that of St. Augustine). Traditional literalism holds that the literal meaning of many scriptural passages can be saved in only a general sense via careful interpretation and exegesis, *not* that the "surface meaning" is true.

machina mundi: Literally, "the machine of the world," a conception of the universe as a giant mechanism which operates in orderly and predictable ways. The concept of the *machina mundi* began to emerge in the Middle Ages, but became strongest in the 17th century within the concept of the mechanical philosophy.

Manicheanism: Strictly speaking, a religious movement based on the teachings of the Persian self-styled prophet Manes and containing a farrago of notions drawn from astral religions, Zoroastrianism, and Christianity. Main tenets include dualism—the constant conflict between good and evil forces/deities—the belief that matter is evil. As a heretical movement, it was popular in parts of the Roman world in the patristic period (it seduced St. Augustine in his youth), and in various altered forms, it has continued to erupt occasionally in various locales; the mindset of American fundamentalism is substantially Manichean.

materialism: The view that material substance is all that exists—no soul, no spirits, no God.

mechanical philosophy: A collection of worldviews popular in the 17th century, characterized by the vision of the world as a machine in which the sole basis for natural phenomena was matter and motion.

monogenism: The position that all human beings are related by virtue of being descended from a single common ancestor. **See polygenism.**

natural theology: The use of the natural world as a source of information about God and his attributes. Although the belief that the natural world could reveal something about God dates to Classical antiquity (and before Christianity, for example, in Cicero), a distinct "natural theology" appeared only in the late 17th century, largely in Protestant contexts, and was popular predominantly in England in the 18th and 19th centuries. Compare **design argument**.

naturalism: The use of natural forces alone to explain the causation of phenomena. It is important to distinguish *methodological naturalism* from *philosophical naturalism*. The former is one of the fundamental "rules of the game" of modern science (and the general tendency of medieval natural philosophy and theology, as well) and holds only that we are not allowed to invoke divine interventions as explanations of things we do not understand. It makes *no* claims about the existence of God or his interventions in the world, only that it is not acceptable to use such as explanations in a scientific context. Philosophical naturalism, however, is a more radical view that denies the existence of anything supernatural (that is, "above nature"). All philosophical naturalists are, by definition, methodological naturalists, but not all methodological naturalists are philosophical naturalists.

normative: Ideas or notions that are set down as a rule or norm and endeavor to make claims about the way things should be.

occasionalism: A philosophical position that holds that natural objects have no inherent causative power, that the connections we see between cause and effect are merely apparent, and that effects are actually the direct result of divine activity. In other words, there is no secondary causation.

philosophers' stone: A substance prepared in the alchemical laboratory by a secret process that, when cast upon a quantity of molten metal, transmutes it in a few minutes into pure gold (or silver). The philosophers' stone is first mentioned in the writings of Hellenistic Egypt (c. A.D. 300) and was a chief pursuit of alchemists down to the 18th century.

polygenism: The position that there are several distinct and unrelated races within the human species as the result of descent from several different ancestors. A position condemned by the Catholic Church. **See monogenism.**

primary causation: Causation that stems directly from the First Cause, that is, God (see **secondary causation**).

rationalism: The view that everything in existence is accessible to and explicable by human reason.

realism: A view that holds that our scientific theories and explanations are (or should be) literally true descriptions of reality ("the way things really are"). Compare **instrumentalism**.

recta fides: Literally "right faith"; namely, the belief in things in which it is correct or proper to believe, as opposed simply to indiscriminate belief.

recta ratio: Literally "right reason"; namely, rational methods applied correctly and fitly. Since human reason can often lead to false conclusions, there must be a distinction between its proper and improper usages.

scientism: A view that exalts the status of science and scientific inquiry (of course, in the modern, current, Western sense of the word) to an absolutely predominant position, capable of solving, explaining, and/or passing judgment on everything. In some cases, it is equivalent to science as religion.

secondary causation: Causation that stems from any created (secondary) cause, that is, from anything other than God (see **primary causation**).

supernaturalism: The use of supernatural forces and interventions to explain the causation of phenomena.

theistic evolution: The position that evolution has been, in some sense, guided by God. The degrees of "guidance" envisioned span a vast range, from multiple direct intercessions (primary causations) to create new species or variants to a chain of secondary causations (either necessary or contingent) stretching back through billions of years to a single, initial primary causation at the moment of creation.

theology: The rational and intellectual study of God, his attributes, activities, and relationship to the creation.

Biographical Notes

St. Augustine of Hippo (354–430): Probably the most influential and important Christian theologian of all time. Born at Tagaste in North Africa (currently in Tunisia) of a Christian mother and pagan father, Augustine studied philosophy and rhetoric at Carthage; went to Rome and Milan, where he was baptized; then returned to North Africa, where he became bishop of Hippo and founded a monastery. A prolific and highly learned writer whose voluminous works were well known and esteemed throughout the Middle Ages (and down to the present day among the *cognoscenti*), he effected a powerful synthesis of Christianity and Greek philosophical thought, oversaw important Church councils, and laid the foundations for the accepted methods of biblical interpretation.

Bellarmino, St. Roberto (1542–1621): A native of Montepulciano in Tuscany, Bellarmino distinguished himself as the preeminent theologian of the Counter-Reformation. He studied at the Jesuit college of his hometown and entered the Jesuit Society in 1560. He then studied at Rome, Padua (1567–1569), and Louvain (from 1569); returned to Italy in 1576; and became a member of the Collegio Romano. He was made cardinal in 1599 and bishop of Capua in 1602; at the conclave of 1605, he was advanced as a candidate for pope, but he refused to accept. Bellarmino dealt with Galileo, with whom he was on friendly terms, during the first phase of his inquiry (1612–1616). He gave away all his goods to the poor and died a pauper. His canonization occurred in the early 20th century.

Bentley, Richard (1662–1742): Born in Yorkshire, Bentley was educated at Cambridge (B.A., 1680; M.A., 1683), took Anglican Holy Orders in 1690, and became Keeper of the Royal Library in 1693, Fellow of the Royal Society in 1695, and D.D. in 1696. In 1700, he became master of Trinity College, Cambridge (Newton's college). His best known work is as a Classicist, but he was also the first Boyle lecturer (1692–1695), where he used scientific information gleaned from Newton in the defense of revealed religion.

Boyle, Robert (1627–1691): Seventh son and fourteenth child of the wealthy Richard, Great Earl of Cork. Boyle was schooled at Eton and tutored during a Continental Grand Tour. His first career was as a moralist, but around 1650, his interests turned to natural philosophy. He relocated to Oxford in the mid-1650s, where he participated in an "Experimental Club." There, he set the foundations of his scientific career. Boyle later moved to London and took up residence with his sister, with whom he lived the rest of his life. He helped found the Royal Society in 1660, published a book (either on science or theology) nearly every year after 1659, and became the most celebrated natural philosopher in Britain. Unlike Newton, he was of a pleasant disposition and highly charitable and maintained correspondence with hundreds of savants across Europe. He was offered the presidency of the Royal Society, the knighthood, and ordination as a bishop, but he refused. His legacy funds an annual lecture on Christianity and, in the early years, supported an "Indian college" at William and Mary.

Buffon, Georges-Louis Leclerc, Comte de (1707–1788): An important French naturalist, member of the Académie Royale des Sciences and other learned societies, and head of the Jardin du Roi from 1739. His interests ranged over botany, mathematics, and mechanics. His most famous work is the 36-volume *Histoire naturelle*. He also proposed an origin for the solar system in the *solar ejecta* following the collision of a comet with the Sun.

Burnet, Thomas (c. 1635–1715): Educated at Cambridge and ordained an Anglican priest, Burnet's claim to fame is his authorship of *A Sacred Theory of the Earth*, first published in Latin in 1681, then in English in 1684, and revised and expanded thereafter. This work endeavored to work out a geology and chronology of the Earth from creation to the final conflagration and to explain geological observations in terms of biblical events. It was criticized at the time on both scientific and exegetical grounds.

Caccini, Tommaso (1574–1648): A minor Dominican friar at Santa Maria Novella in Florence who preached a sermon against mathematicians in general and Galileo in particular on the fourth Sunday of Advent in 1614. His superior apologized to Galileo for the incident. He had previously been disciplined by the archbishop of Bologna as a troublemaker.

Castelli, Benedetto (1578–1643): Born in Brescia, Castelli entered the Benedictine order in 1595 and studied with Galileo in Padua from about 1604 to 1607. Castelli helped Galileo in various activities, including his publications and solar observations. Galileo recommended Castelli for the chair of mathematics at the University of Padua, and the two remained fast friends. In 1626, Castelli moved to Rome as a consultant on river management and professor of mathematics. He wrote on hydraulics, optics and vision, and other subjects.

Copernicus, Nicolaus (1473–1543): Born in Torun, Poland, Nicolaus was orphaned young and raised by his uncle, the bishop of Warmia. He studied at Krakow (1491–1495) first, then canon and civil law and medicine in Italy. He received the post of canon at Frauenburg from his uncle in 1497, where he took up residence (for the rest of his life) in 1510. He is best known for advancing the heliocentric theory, presented in his book *De revolutionibus* (1543).

Descartes, René (1596–1650): Born at La Haye, Descartes was educated at the Jesuit college of La Flèche (1606–1614), then studied law at Poitiers (1614–1615). He left France for the Netherlands, where he conducted further personal studies, wrote and published profusely, and corresponded widely. His natural philosophical system attracted numerous adherents for a century, and his mathematical innovations (for example, Cartesian coordinates) continue to be fundamental.

Draper, John William (1811–1882): Born in England, Draper emigrated to the United States, where he received an M.D. at the University of Pennsylvania and became a professor of chemistry, researching light and its chemical activity (including photography). He was elected president of the American Chemical Society. He turned to historical writing (embracing positivism) and wrote the enormously popular *History of the Conflict between Religion and Science* (1874), from whose erroneous claims, false assumptions, and melodrama we are not yet free more than a century later.

Eichhorn, Johann Gottfried (1752–1827): Eichhorn has been called the "father of modern Old Testament criticism," that is, higher criticism. Born in Germany and educated at Göttingen, he became professor of oriental languages at Jena in 1775. In 1778, he moved to a professorship at Göttingen, where he lectured on oriental languages, exegesis, and political history. He treated the Bible as an ancient text open to all the critical tools of the scholar. Among his most important discoveries was the multiple authorship within the Pentateuch, or Books of Moses.

Foscarini, Paolo Antonio (1565–1616): Foscarini was a native of Calabria and joined the Carmelite Order. He taught philosophy and theology at the University of Messina and published on devotion, doctrine, divination, and cosmology. He founded a Carmelite monastery in his hometown of Montalto. Foscarini's interest in the Copernican system resulted in a book entitled *Lettera sopra l'Opinione de' Pittagorici, e del Copernico della Mobilità della Terra, e Stabilità del Sole, e del Nuove Pittagorica Systema del Mondo* (*Letter about the Opinion of the Pythagoreans and of Copernicus Concerning the Mobility of the Earth and the Stability of the Sun, and about the New Pythagorean System of the World*), published in 1615 during the first phase of the Galileo affair. The book, which gave new interpretations of Scripture designed to fit the Copernican system, was prohibited by the Index in 1616.

Galilei, Galileo (1564–1642): Born the son of Vincenzo Galilei, a noted composer and music theorist, Galileo began his education at the University of Pisa in 1580 but left without a degree in 1585. After work on Archimedean hydrostatics and the vibration of strings, he returned to Pisa in the chair of mathematics in 1589 and moved to Padua in 1592. After his celestial discoveries of 1609, Cosimo de' Medici gave him a sinecure chair at Pisa and a position as philosopher and mathematician in his Florentine court. In 1615, Galileo was questioned by the Inquisition and, although found not guilty of the original (serious) charges, was told not to teach Copernicanism as literally true. After a series of complicated events, Galileo was questioned again in 1633 and shown to have transgressed the ruling of 1616; he recanted the notion of terrestrial motion and remained under house arrest at his villa in Florence the rest of his life, during which time he wrote arguably his most important book, *Two New Sciences*.

Gassendi, Pierre (1592–1655): Gassendi was born in Provence, entered the priesthood, studied at Aix-en-Provence, then earned a doctorate in theology at Avignon in 1614. In 1634, he became provost of the cathedral of Digne and was appointed professor of mathematics at the Collège Royal in 1645. His massive natural philosophical work, the *Syntagma philosophica* (aimed at replacing Aristotelianism with a revived atomic philosophy) was published posthumously in 1658.

Halley, Edmond (1656–1742): Halley was born in London and attended Oxford starting in 1673. He voyaged to St. Helena to study the stars of the southern hemisphere. He was elected Fellow of the Royal Society in 1678, became Savilian Professor of geometry in

1704, and Astronomer Royal in 1721. He is best known for his work on comets, notably predicting the return of the great comet of 1680 in 1756, a comet that ever since has borne his name.

Hodge, Charles (1797–1878): This influential Presbyterian theologian was principal of Princeton Theological Seminary from 1851 to 1878. He wrote extensively, embracing a conservative interpretation of Calvinist doctrine. His 1874 book *What Is Darwinism?* equated Darwinism with atheism.

John Paul II (1920–2005): Born Karol Jósef Wojtyla in Wadowice, Poland, he entered the seminary in Krakow (then meeting secretly, owing to the Nazi occupation) in 1942, was ordained priest in 1946, and received the doctorate in theology in 1948. A professor at Lublin University, he became a bishop in 1958, archbishop of Krakow in 1964, cardinal in 1967, and on 16 October 1978, the 263rd successor to Peter as the first Polish pope. His pontificate lasted 27 years, the third longest in history, during which time he held more than 1,160 general audiences, oversaw the Jubilee of the Third Millennium, made innumerable speeches and statements, issued a large number of important teaching documents, created 231 cardinals, proclaimed 1,338 *beati* and 482 saints, traveled more than all previous pontiffs combined, and revised numerous Church mechanisms.

Kepler, Johannes (1571–1630): Kepler was born in Weil-der-Stadt, Württenberg, to a poor but noble family. He began seminary at Adelberg in 1584, but his talents enabled him to go on to the University of Tübingen in 1588, where he studied with Michael Maestlin. He accepted the job of astronomy lecturer at Graz in 1594. In 1600, he went to work with Tycho Brahe, who had recently transferred to Rudolf II's court in Prague; when Tycho died in 1601, Kepler inherited his post as imperial mathematician. For 12 years, he lived at Linz and was invited to London by James I and to a chair at Bologna but declined both. Kepler's life was fraught with problems from the outset: His parents became bankrupt, his wife and three children died young, his mother was tried as a witch, his salary was rarely paid, and he seemed always caught in sectarian crossfire.

Lemaître, Georges (1894–1966): The "father of Big-Bang cosmology" was born in Charleroi, Belgium; studied humanities at a Jesuit school; volunteered in the Belgian army in 1914; and after the armistice, began studies of physics and mathematics and for the priesthood. He received a Ph.D. in 1920 and was ordained in 1923.

In the same year, he studied with Arthur Eddington at Cambridge, then with Shapley at Harvard, and finally, at the Massachusetts Institute of Technology. He returned to Belgium in 1925 and, in 1927, published a paper containing arguments for an expanding universe; his views were accepted only slowly, but he won over Einstein in 1935. Later in life, Lemaître was involved with computer development. He received numerous distinctions both Belgian and international, including membership in the Pontifical Academy of Sciences (1936), and was the president of that body from 1960.

Lorini, Niccolò (dates unknown): A minor Dominican friar at Santa Maria Novella in Florence. Wrote a letter of complaint against Galileo and his followers to the Inquisition, thus precipitating the Galileo affair.

Mersenne, Marin (1588–1648): Although initially a religious writer and supporter of Aristotle, Mersenne became one of the most important researchers and promoters of the "New Science" of the 17th century. He advocated a mathematical approach to nature and created a huge correspondence network and academy for the exchange of scientific ideas. A Minim friar from 1611 and priest from 1612, Mersenne was also a staunch supporter of Galileo by the early 1630s. He studied acoustics, mathematics, the speed of sound, the barometer, falling bodies, and other topics; encouraged other scholars, including Gassendi, Descartes, and Huygens; and published prolifically.

Mivart, Saint George Jackson (1827–1900): A Londoner by birth and a convert to Catholicism in 1844, Mivart became a noted anatomist and biologist. He studied under Huxley, beginning in 1859, and became a Fellow of the Royal Society. His best-known work is the 1871 *On the Genesis of Species*, which adopts evolution but not natural selection as the mechanism (a typical response of scientists of the period) and preserves the transcendence of the human soul. Late in life, Mivart espoused views that brought him into conflict with Cardinal Vaughan, who excommunicated him in 1900 (but *not* on the grounds of having adopted evolution, as is sometimes claimed).

Newton, Sir Isaac (1642–1727): Son of a yeoman farmer, Newton studied at Cambridge from 1661 to 1665; became Lucasian Chair of Mathematics in 1669, Fellow of the Royal Society in 1671, Master of the Mint in 1696, and president of the Royal Society in 1703; and received a knighthood in 1705. His discoveries in calculus, optics, and celestial motion date from the 1660s. His famed *Principia* was published in 1687 at the urging of Edmond Halley and was followed by texts on optics, ancient chronology, and prophecy. By all accounts, Newton was a difficult and occasionally erratic man.

Paley, William (1743–1805): Born in Peterborough, Paley attended Christ College, Cambridge, where he received his degree in 1763, became a fellow in 1766, and a lecturer in 1768. His lectures dealt primarily with moral philosophy but also with metaphysics and the New Testament. He was ordained in 1767 and was an active opponent of the slave trade. He excelled as a writer of textbooks; thus, his arguments are rarely original but are presented with an elegant and compellingly clear style. His most influential book, *Natural Theology*, was published in 1802 and remained a standard of university curricula for half a century.

Ray, John (1627–1705): Educated at Cambridge in languages, mathematics, and natural science, Ray became an Anglican priest in 1660 and went on travels through England and the Continent collecting flora, fauna, and minerals. He was elected to the Royal Society in 1667. He published widely on scientific and theological topics, promoting biological classification systems and initiating the tradition of English natural theology in 1691 with his *Wisdom of God Manifested in the Works of the Creation*.

Steno, Nicholas (or **Niels Stensen**), **the Blessed** (1638–1686): Steno was born in Copenhagen and became an anatomist. His dissections were renowned for their care and the precision of his observations. After time in Paris, he went to Florence under the patronage of the grand duke of Tuscany. There, he took up a hospital position and membership in the Accademia del Cimento, one of the earliest scientific societies. He turned his attention to fossils and geology and, in 1669, produced his landmark work on rock strata. In 1667, he converted to Catholicism. The Danish king invited him home later that year, but Steno did not go until his freedom of religious practice was guaranteed, which was not forthcoming until 1672. In 1674, he returned to Florence. In 1675, Steno became a priest; in 1677, a bishop; and apostolic vicar to northern Europe. His last years were spent in northern Germany in ceaseless episcopal duties to the Catholic minority and ministry to the poor, and his larger work on strata remained unfinished. In 1988, he was declared a *beatus*; his feast day is 25 November.

Thierry of Chartres (c. 1100–1156): A scholar and teacher at the cathedral school of Chartres. Wrote an important hexameral treatise using Neo-Platonic notions and a commitment to naturalism.

St. Thomas Aquinas (1225–1274): Born in southern Italy, young Thomas was sent to be educated at Monte Cassino. Around 1243, he decided to enter the Dominican Order, to the chagrin of his parents, who apparently imprisoned him for a time to prevent the move. He then studied under St. Albert the Great at Cologne and received degrees at Paris, where he began teaching in 1257. His works included learned commentaries on Aristotle's writings and a host of theological treatises, particularly the comprehensive (but unfinished) *Summa theologiae*. Although some of his theses were initially considered heterodox by some, St. Thomas's work has become central to Catholic theology and has exercised enormous influence on Western philosophy.

Urban VIII (1568–1644): Maffeo Barberini was born into one of the most powerful families of Florence. He received an excellent education from the Jesuits and earned a doctor of laws degree from Pisa in 1589. He became a bishop and cardinal in the first years of the 17th century and was elected pope in 1623. As pope, he was a patron of the arts, encouraged missionary activity, and in 1629, outlawed slavery among the Indians in South America and the West Indies. He had been a friend and supporter of Galileo from at least 1610, but deeply offended and feeling betrayed by Galileo in 1632, Urban pressed for his trial.

White, Andrew Dickson (1832–1918): White had a diverse career as historian, professor, senator, and ambassador. As the co-founder and first president of Cornell University, he received strong criticism for his secular curriculum for the young institution. His response, from 1876 to 1896, was to write and deliver increasingly lengthy (and often rambling) discourses on the "warfare" between science and religion, which though propagandistic and enormously flawed, have had great influence to this day.

William of Conches (c. 1100–1154): Born in Normandy, which he calls "a country of mutton-heads and dense skies," William studied at Chartres under Bernard, then began teaching there himself in the early 1120s. He seems to have had a special interest in natural philosophy. He retired early from the school and became tutor to the sons of Geoffrey Plantagenet (one of whom became England's King Henry II); Geoffrey is one of the interlocutors in William's superb survey of natural philosophy, the *Dragmaticon philosophiae*.

Bibliography

Essential Reading:

Brooke, John Hedley. *Science and Religion: Some Historical Perspectives*. Cambridge: Cambridge University Press, 1991. Excellent work on science and Christianity since the 16th century; chapters on the mechanical universe, the age of the Earth, natural theology, evolution, and more.

Dembski, William A. "Is Intelligent Design a Form of Natural Theology?" Available at www.designinference.com/documents/2001.03.ID_as_nat_theol.htm. Major ID theorist deals with the title question; this document is part of his personal Web site.

Finocchiaro, Maurice A. *The Galileo Affair: A Documentary History*. Berkeley, CA: University of California Press, 1989. The essential work for understanding the Galileo affair; an excellent introduction laying out the issues and chronology. Contains about 250 pages of documents in English translation (including Galileo's pertinent writings and correspondence and all the Inquisition minutes), along with helpful appendices of explanatory notes, biographies, and other material.

International Theological Commission. "Communion and Stewardship." Available at: www.vatican.va/roman_curia/congregations/cfaith/cti_documents/rc_con_cfaith_doc_20040723_communion-stewardship_en.html. Interesting document on man's place in the world; deals with cosmic and biological evolution and environmentalism.

John Paul II. "Address to Pontifical Academy of Sciences" (on evolution). 22 October 1996. Available at: www.ncseweb.org/resources/articles/8712_message_from_the_pope_1996_1_3_2001.asp. Note that the pope spoke in French, and the initially published English translation contained a serious error, officially corrected, that misrepresented the pope's meaning by mistranslating the line "the theory of evolution is more than a hypothesis" as "more than one hypothesis in the theory of evolution." The site listed here gives the correct translation of "*à reconnaître dans la théorie d'évolution plus qu'une hypothèse.*" See also *Quarterly Review of Biology*, below.

————. *Fides et ratio*. Available at: http://www.vatican.va/holy_father/john_paul_ii/encyclicals/documents/hf_jp-ii_enc_14091998_fides-et-ratio_en.html. Encyclical on faith and reason.

Larson, Edward J. *Summer for the Gods: The Scopes Trial and America's Continuing Debate over Science and Religion.* Cambridge, MA: Harvard University Press, 1997. Definitive and Pulitzer Prize–winning work on the Scopes trial.

Lindberg, David C., and Ronald L. Numbers, eds. *God and Nature: Historical Essays on the Encounter between Christianity and Science.* Berkeley, CA: University of California Press, 1986. Eighteen essays by eminent historians ranging over the 20 centuries of Christianity.

Osler, Margaret. "Science and Religion in Early Modern Europe." *History of Science* 36 (1998): 91–113. Argues for the "translation and appropriation" of ideas between science and religion.

Supplementary Reading:

St. Augustine, *Confessions.* R. S. Pine-Coffin, trans. New York: Penguin Books, 1961. Most readable translation of this important work; easily available. Follow St. Augustine on his circuit of the late Classical world. Between the pious exclamations, this book gives a vivid view of the intellectual/philosophical marketplace of A.D. 400 and St. Augustine's real indebtedness to Classical thought.

Brooke, John Hedley, Margaret J. Osler, and Jitse van der Meer. *Science in Theistic Contexts: Cognitive Dimensions* (*Osiris*, vol. 16). Chicago: History of Science Society, 2001. Two introductory essays followed by 14 case studies of science/religion, including Judaism and Islam. Research-level papers from a conference.

Browne, Janet. *Charles Darwin: Voyaging.* Princeton: Princeton University Press, 1995.

———. *Charles Darwin: The Power of Place.* New York: Knopf, 2002. Browne's books are often considered the definitive biographical works on Darwin. The first volume (*Voyaging*) covers the period up to the publication of the *Origin of Species* (1859), while the second takes the story through the rest of Darwin's life. Very readable, engaging, and comprehensive.

Colling, Richard G. *Random Designer.* Bourbonnais, IL: Browning Press, 2004. Book by a microbiologist and conservative Christian who argues that the continuing flap over evolution and creationism is pointless and unnecessary; includes criticisms of intelligent design and the dangers of fundamentalist opposition to science.

Consolmagno, Guy. *Brother Astronomer: Adventures of a Vatican Scientist*. New York: McGraw-Hill, 2001. A popular book written by a Jesuit astronomer currently at the Vatican's Observatory, detailing his science (the study of meteorites), his life, and personal reflections on science and religion.

Cutler, Alan. *The Seashell on the Mountaintop*. New York: Dutton, 2003. Very readable popular book on the life and work of (the Blessed) Nicholas Steno, aka Niels Stensen.

Draper, John William. *A History of the Conflict between Religion and Science*. New York: Appleton, 1876. (Many later editions exist.) The book that started the conflict myth. Take a sense of humor and/or a stiff drink with this dated bit of melodrama.

Ferngren, Gary B., ed. *The History of Science and Religion in the Western Tradition*: *An Encyclopedia*. New York: Garland, 2000. An outstanding resource—more than 100 articles on various aspects of the science/religion issue. Much more than an "encyclopedia"; every entry is highly readable and informative. A fast and effective method of learning about a great many aspects of the topic.

Fleming, Donald H. *John William Draper and the Religion of Science*. New York: Octagon Books, 1972. The only book-length treatment of Draper; now a bit dated in some respects but with excellent use of archival material.

Funkenstein, Amos. *Theology and the Scientific Imagination from the Middle Ages to the Seventeenth Century*. Princeton: Princeton University Press, 1986. A masterful treatment of the impact of theological ideas and methods on scientific ones, including Christianity, Islam, and Judaism. A high-level text, it can be a difficult read, but it is a classic.

Gould, Stephen J. *Rocks of Ages: Science and Religion in the Fullness of Life*. New York: Ballantine, 1999. The author presents his NOMA formulation in this popular book.

Halley, Edmund. "Some Considerations about the Deluge." *Philosophical Transactions of the Royal Society of London* (1694): 118–123. Halley's suggestion that the collision of a comet with the Earth caused the axial tilt and Noah's Flood.

Howell, Kenneth J. *God's Two Books: Copernican Cosmology and Biblical Interpretation in Early Modern Science*. Notre Dame, IN: Notre Dame Press, 2002. Definitive work on the wide varieties of biblical interpretation—Catholic and Protestant—of the 16th and early 17th centuries and the relationship to the new cosmology of Copernicus. Essential background to the Galileo affair.

Kragh, Helge. *Cosmology and Controversy: The Historical Development of Two Theories of the Universe*. Princeton: Princeton University Press, 1996. Excellent coverage of the steady-state versus Big-Bang models of the universe. Deals predominantly with the scientific issues but includes a few sections on the theological impacts of each.

Lindberg, David C., and Ronald L. Numbers. "Beyond War and Peace: A Reappraisal of the Encounter between Christianity and Science." *Church History* 55 (1986): 338–354. Critique of White's warfare model.

————, eds. *When Science and Christianity Meet*. Chicago: University of Chicago Press, 2003. Collection of 12 essays by eminent scholars on Christianity and science from the patristic period to the 20th century. Similar to *God and Nature* by the same editors.

Livingstone, David N., and Mark A. Noll. "B. B. Warfield (1851–1921): A Biblical Inerrantist as Evolutionist." *Isis* 91 (2000): 283–304. Scholarly article on the developing evolutionary views of one of the main crafters of the doctrine of biblical inerrancy.

Marsden, George M. *Understanding Fundamentalism and Evangelicalism*. Grand Rapids, MI: Eerdmans, 1991. Definitive, highly readable work on the subject by the leading historian of the topic.

Numbers, Ronald L. *Darwinism Comes to America*. Cambridge, MA: Harvard University Press, 1998. Short survey of American attitudes to Darwinism (pro, con, and in the middle), how they evolved, and why.

————. *The Creationists*. New York: Knopf, 1992. Fascinating account of the rise of fundamentalism and allied creationism in the United States; highly detailed and written with an engrossing narrative style.

Principe, Lawrence M. *Aspiring Adept*. Princeton: Princeton University Press, 1998. A work predominantly on Boyle's interests in alchemy, but it also treats his interest in contacting angels and contains a transcription of his unpublished dialogue on communication with spirits using the philosophers' stone and how this is related to refuting atheism.

Quarterly Review of Biology. "The Pope's Message on Evolution and Four Commentaries." December 1997. (Available as a single issue from *Quarterly Review of Biology*, P. O. Box 37005, University of Chicago Press, Chicago, IL 60637.) French and English text of John Paul II's statement on evolution (see note under John Paul II, "Address," above), plus interesting comments from an ethicist, a historian/philosopher of science, and a science educator and an embarrassingly ignorant but mercifully short rant by Richard Dawkins.

Ross, Hugh. *A Matter of Days.* Colorado Springs. CO: Navpress, 2004. A publication by an evangelical striving to debunk Young-Earth creationism and a literal six-days interpretation of creation while still denying evolution. Not a historical work, but an example of the cross-currents among present-day biblical inerrantists.

Scott, Eugenie C. *Creationism vs. Evolution: An Introduction.* Westport, CT: Greenwood Press, 2004. A useful survey of the issues and history regarding current-day arguments; written in particular for schoolteachers.

Tompkins, J. R. *D-Days at Dayton: Reflections on the Scopes Trial.* Baton Rouge: Louisiana State University Press, 1965. Out of print, but borrow a copy especially to read the collected dispatches from the trial by the curmudgeonly Sage of Baltimore, H. L. Mencken.

William of Conches. *A Dialogue on Natural Philosophy* (*Dragmaticon Philosophiae*). Italo Ronca and Matthew Curr, eds. South Bend, IN: University of Notre Dame Press, 1997. A very readable translation that provides a fine sense of the use of *naturalism* in medieval natural philosophy.

Notes

Notes